OUR LIFE IN CHRIST

Adult Study Guide

Book 2

By Thomas J. Doyle

Portions of the "Inform" and "Connect" Sections Were
Written by David Adams and Kenneth Wagener

CPH
SAINT LOUIS

Write to the Library for the Blind, 1333 S. Kirkwood Road, St. Louis, MO 63122-7295 to obtain this study in braille or large print for the visually impaired.

Quotations from the Small Catechism are from *Luther's Small Catechism with Explanation.* Copyright © 1986, 1991 by Concordia Publishing House. All rights reserved.

Scripture quotations taken from the HOLY BIBLE: NEW INTERNATIONAL VERSION®. NIV®. Copyright © 1973, 1978, 1984 by International Bible Society. Used by permission of Zondervan Publishing House. All rights reserved.

Copyright © 1997 Concordia Publishing House
3558 South Jefferson Avenue, St. Louis, MO 63118-3968
Manufactured in the United States of America

2   3   4   5   6   7   8   9   10   06   05   04   03   02   01   00   99   98   97

Contents

Introduction

God promises to strengthen our life in Christ as we study His Word. The Our Life in Christ Bible study series provides you resources to help you study God's Word. The series gives you an opportunity to study in-depth some familiar, and possibly, not-so-familiar Bible stories.

Each of the 9 Bible study books has 13 sessions that are divided into 4 easy-to-use sections.

Focus—Section 1 of each session focuses the participant's attention on the key concept that will be discovered in the session.

Inform—Section 2 explores a portion of Scripture through the use of a brief commentary and through discussion questions that help the participant study the text.

Connect—Section 3 helps the participant apply God's Law and Gospel as revealed in the scriptural account to their lives.

Vision—Section 4 provides the participants with practical suggestions for taking the theme of the lesson out of the classroom and into their families.

Our Life in Christ is designed to assist both novice and expert Bible students in their study of Holy Scripture. It offers resources that will enable them to grow in their understanding of God's Word while strengthening their life in Christ.

As an added benefit, the sessions in the Our Life in Christ adult Bible study series follow the Scripture lessons taught in the Our Life in Christ Sunday school series. Parents will enjoy studying in-depth the Bible stories their children are studying in Sunday school. This will provide parents and children additional opportunities to

- discuss God's Word together;
- apply lesson applications to everyday situations;
- pray together;
- engage in family activities that grow out of lesson truths.

We pray that as you study God's Word using the Our Life in Christ Bible study series, your life in Christ may be strengthened.

Session 1

John Prepares the Way for Jesus

(Malachi 3:1–4; Luke 1:57–60; 3:1–6)

Focus

Theme: Called to Repentance

Law/Gospel Focus

Because of sin no one is able to stand in God's presence. All would be eternally separated from God. But God in His love for all people sends messengers to call people to repentance and faith in Jesus. Through Word and Sacrament these messengers proclaim the Good News of pardon and peace through Jesus Christ, our Savior and Lord.

Objectives

By the power of the Holy Spirit working through God's Word we will
1. confess our sinfulness and need for a Savior;
2. compare the messages of the Old Testament prophet Malachi and John the Baptizer;
3. identify messengers sent by God to proclaim God's Law and God's Gospel;
4. give thanks to God for His messengers and His message proclaimed by them.

Opening Worship

Read responsively Isaiah 40:1–8.
Leader: Comfort, comfort My people says your God.
Participants: Speak tenderly to Jerusalem, and proclaim to her that her hard service has been completed, that her sin has been paid for, that she has received from the LORD's hand double for all her sins.

Leader: A voice of one calling: "In the desert prepare the way for the LORD; make straight in the wilderness a highway for our God.

Participants: Every valley shall be raised up, every mountain and hill made low; the rough ground shall become level, and rugged places a plain.

Leader: And the glory of the LORD will be revealed, and all mankind together will see it. For the mouth of the LORD has spoken.

Participants: A voice says, "Cry out." And I said, "What shall I cry?" "All men are like grass, and all their glory is like the flowers of the field.

Leader: The grass withers and the flowers fall, because the breath of the LORD blows on them. Surely the people are grass.

Participants: The grass withers and the flowers fall, but the Word of our God stands forever."

All: Amen.

Introduction

At times we have all received a message from someone. Think back to some messages you have received.

1. Share the worst message you have ever received.

2. What made this message the worst?

3. Share the best message you have ever received.

4. What made this message the best?

Today, we will examine messages sent from God—bad and good—but always with one purpose—to cause people to examine their lives, repent of their sinfulness, and receive the forgiveness God desires to provide through His Son's death on the cross.

Inform

Reading the Text

Read aloud Malachi 3:1–4; Luke 1:57–60, 3:1–6.

Like many other Old Testament men and women, the prophet Malachi's name has special significance for his life and mission. Malachi was God's messenger. (Malachi means "my messenger.") Sometime after the rebuilding of the Jerusalem temple in 515 B.C., God called Malachi to speak His word of righteous indignation and judgment upon the nation of Israel.

Years before (538 B.C.), God had brought His chosen people home after a long exile in Babylon. Hundreds of families made the long journey back to Jerusalem, eager to rebuild the temple and begin a new life under God's care and blessing. In time, though, the joy and gratitude faded away. Religious leaders and people alike fell into apathy and unfaithfulness. Worship at the temple was superficial: priests offered "injured, crippled or diseased animals" as sacrifices, even though God required an "unblemished" animal (1:13–14). Divorce was common and simple: men and women "broke faith" with their marriage covenant (2:14). In general, the people of Israel were overcome by pessimism and unbelief: "Where is the God of justice?" (2:17). Many felt isolated, abandoned by God, and surrounded by foes and hardships.

In response, Malachi announces an extraordinary promise from God: The Lord is coming to His people! "I will send My messenger who will prepare the way before Me" (3:1). Like Isaiah centuries before (Isaiah 40:1–5), Malachi proclaims that the living God, the God of the covenant, will come to restore and renew His people. Before His arrival, though, God sends His chosen servant, an envoy who summons His people to repentance and faith. "Prepare the Lord's way!" is the messenger's cry, for the "day of the Lord" is near.

Yet the Lord, too, is a messenger; he is the "messenger of the covenant" (Malachi 3:1), the one who proclaims, establishes, and seals God's new covenant of forgiveness, life, and salvation. The Lord comes to His temple to reveal His mercy and power to His chosen people.

But His people are sinful. They are impure, like precious gold and silver mixed with worthless metals. They are unclean, like a white garment soiled with dirt and grime. On their own, God's people cannot stand in His presence, for He is the Holy One of Israel, the righteous King. In truth, no one "can endure the day of His coming" (v. 2). All humankind is guilty before the Lord.

Only the Lord can cleanse His people from their sin. Israel's Father will once more redeem His children from slavery, refining and purifying both the priests and the people in His mercy and compassion. The Lord is "the messenger of the covenant" (v. 1), who restores the holy relationship broken long ago by human sinfulness (see Jeremiah 31:31–34). Living in grace, His people are made new, able to offer acceptable sacrifices to their Savior God (v. 4).

Nearly 500 years later, God fulfills His promise to send His messenger to "prepare the way of the Lord" in the birth of John the Baptizer. A gift of God's grace (John means "God is gracious"), John has a unique role in the unfolding drama of redemption. By God's design, he goes on "before the Lord, in the spirit and power of Elijah, to turn the hearts of the fathers to their children ... to make ready a people prepared for the Lord" (Luke 1:17; see also Malachi 4:5–6). John is the forerunner, the herald of God's promised Messiah; as a prophet, he is a witness to the coming Christ, who inaugurates the new covenant of forgiveness and peace with God through His death and resurrection.

John's distinctive role is to call all people to repentance, preaching God's righteous law and baptizing with water for the forgiveness of sins (Luke 3:3). In John's mission, the words of the ancient prophets—Malachi and Isaiah especially—are fulfilled.

John is like Elijah, a prophet whose manner of life reflects the priority and urgency of God's mission to the world. His clothing is unpretentious, his diet austere. A simple thought dominates his preaching: Christ is at hand. And John properly recognizes his secondary role in the story of salvation. He is the messenger. "One more powerful" comes afterward, and in contrast John is lower than the lowest servant. He is unworthy to kneel and untie the Messiah's sandals (see Luke 3:16–18).

John's baptism, though valid as a baptism of repentance for forgiveness, is the spark that finds fulfillment in Baptism with water and the Spirit (John 3:5). Jesus pours out the Spirit on His people in a decisive way. In Christian Baptism, the Spirit of God generates faith, washes away sin and guilt, and empowers for a life of witness and service. John's great joy is the knowledge that the Messiah will bring to pass all of God's ancient promises to save His people—completely and with almighty power.

Discussing the Text

1. What "bad" message did both Malachi and John share with the people?

2. What "good" message did both Malachi and John share with the people?

3. How was the "bad" message of sin really a "good" message for the people to hear?

4. What is the distinctive role of both John and Malachi?

Connect

"Who can stand in God's presence?" Both Malachi and John know that human beings can only cower in fear before the holy, majestic, eternal God. In the light of the divine Law, our sinfulness and need for salvation is all too apparent. We can only kneel in repentance, crying out for forgiveness in utter humility. The Good News, however, proclaims that God has delivered us from sin, death, and Satan. Jesus invites us to stand before our loving Father. His life, death, and resurrection are the one divinely appointed means for full forgiveness and life eternal.

Today, too, God sends His messengers to call people to repentance and faith in Christ. Through Word and Sacrament, pastors and teachers share the good news of pardon and peace through Jesus, our Savior and Lord.

1. How does God call people to repentance and faith in Jesus today?

2. God speaks through His Word
- Law—the "bad" news that we are sinners and because of our sin we deserve to die.
- Gospel—the "good" news that because of His love for us God sent His only Son, Jesus, to live a perfect life on our behalf and then suffered the punishment we deserved because of our sin. Jesus won for us forgiveness of sins and eternal life.

Why are these messages so important for people to hear today?

3. What danger do people face if they fail to heed the message of the Law? See Romans 6:23a.

4. What does God continue to provide to repentant sinners today? See Romans 6:23b and Romans 8:1–4.

5. How can God use you as one of His messengers?

Vision

To Do This Week
Family Connection
1. Discuss the messages of Malachi and John.
2. Why is it good for parents to teach their children right and wrong?
3. How do parents demonstrate their love for their children when they correct their children for doing wrong? forgive their children when they express sorrow for these wrong things they do?
4. How might we speak the truth in love?

Personal Reflection
1. Consider how the "bad" news and the "good" news are both provided to us in love.
2. Think about new ways you can share the God's message with someone you love. Then do it.
3. Pray for those who have rejected God's call to repentance. Pray that the Holy Spirit would transform their hearts as they hear the message of God's love for them in Christ Jesus.

Closing Worship
Pray together the Confession.

Leader: Let us confess our sins to God the Father.

Participants: Most merciful God, we confess that we are by nature sinful and unclean. We have sinned against You in thought, word, and deed, by what we have done and by what we have left undone. We have not loved You with our whole heart; we have not loved our neighbors as ourselves. We justly deserve Your present and eternal punishment. For the sake of Your Son, Jesus Christ, have mercy on us. Forgive us, renew us, and lead us, so that we may delight in Your will and walk in Your ways to the glory of Your holy name. Amen.

Leader: In the mercy of almighty God, Jesus Christ was given to die for us, and for His sake God forgives us all our sins. To those who believe in Jesus Christ He gives the power to become the children of God and bestows on them the Holy Spirit. May the Lord, who has begun this good work in us, bring it to completion in the day of our Lord Jesus Christ.

For Next Week

Read Zephaniah 3:14–18; Luke 1:39–55; and Philippians 4:4–9 in preparation for the next session.

Session 2

The Savior Brings Joy

(Zephaniah 3:14–18; Luke 1:39–55; Philippians 4:4–9)

Focus

Theme: The Great Reversal

Law/Gospel Focus

Because of sin, people were guilty before God and deserved the punishment of death. But God in His love for all people designed a loving plan to rescue His people. God would send His only Son, Jesus, to this earth to do that which sinful people could never do—keep God's Law by living a sinless, perfect life. And then in a great act of reversal, sinless Jesus would receive the punishment we deserved because of our sin by dying on the cross. Through Jesus' life and death God would provide us life eternal. In His resurrection Jesus proclaims for us the victory He won over death. Through Jesus we are able to confess with Mary, "for the Mighty One has done great things for me" (Luke 1:49).

Objectives

By the power of the Holy Spirit working through God's Word we will

1. confess our sinfulness for which we deserve death;
2. rejoice in the forgiveness God won for us through Jesus' life, death, and resurrection;
3. praise God for His words of judgment that show us our sin and our need for a savior, and for God's words of mercy that show us our Savior;
4. write our own magnificat that proclaims the wonders of God's work in our lives by His grace through faith in Jesus.

Opening Worship

Read responsively Mary's song of praise from Luke 1:46–55.

Leader: "My soul glorifies the Lord and my spirit rejoices in God my Savior,

Participants: For He has been mindful of the humble state of His servant. From now on all generations will call me blessed,

Leader: For the Mighty One has done great things for me— holy is His name.

Participants: His mercy extends to those who fear Him from generation to generation.

Leader: He has performed mighty deeds with His arm; He has scattered those who are proud in their inmost thoughts.

Participants: He has brought down rulers from their thrones but has lifted up the humble.

Leader: He has filled the hungry with good things but has sent the rich away empty.

Participants: He has helped His servant Israel, remembering to be merciful to Abraham and his descendants forever, even as He said to our fathers." Amen.

Introduction

John was sick of his job. Angelique was unfulfilled in her role as wife and mother. Numerous arguments concerning whose job was more difficult had escalated to the point where John resented Angelique's "freedom to do whatever she wanted during the day." Angelique coveted John's ability to be out with other adults "performing meaningful activity." One Sunday evening after a bitter fight John and Angelique agreed to reverse roles. John would stay at home and care for the children and Angelique would get a job outside of the home.

1. What are some possible endings to the story?

2. Share some other "reversals" you have heard of or experienced.

God provided a great reversal for us in the person and through the work of Jesus. In this great reversal Jesus received the punishment we deserved because of sin—death—and we received by God's grace through faith that which on our own we could never earn—eternal life. In today's lesson we learn of the fulfillment of God's great plan of reversal as we witness the incarnation of God's holy, sinless Son, "conceived by the Holy Spirit, born of the Virgin Mary," and the young virgin's response to this divine miracle.

Inform

Reading the Text

Read aloud Zephaniah 3:14–18; Luke 1:39–55; and Philippians 4:4–9.

Zephaniah spoke God's Word to the people of Judah during the early years of king Josiah's rule (around 640 B.C.). Though a descendant of royalty and a prominent member of society, Zephaniah's mission was to bring a startling rebuke to his beloved Jerusalem: guilty! God's people were guilty. They stood under divine judgment for their utter disregard of God's truth and their rebellion against His will. Defiance. Arrogance. Treachery. These were now the marks of the nation's social and spiritual life. In truth, Jerusalem was ready to collapse under the weight of rampant idolatry and willful disobedience.

God's declaration of judgment was, then, swift and severe: "I will sweep away everything from the face of the earth" (Zephaniah 1:2). As in the days of Noah, God reveals His will to destroy life on earth, a tragic indication of the depth of Judah's sin and disobedience.

But judgment is not the prophet's only message from God. In mercy, God promises a joyous future for His chosen people. "Sing … shout aloud … Be glad and rejoice" (3:14) are the marks of a festival celebration. The Lord, "the King of Israel" (3:15), invites the nation to trust His power to save, even after He disciplines His unruly children. What will God do for His people? Take away their punishment! turn back their enemy! protect them from harm! (v. 15). Though they suffer hardship for a while—a hardship brought on by their sinfulness—

17

God's people will find strength and comfort in His salvation.

"The LORD your God is with you, He is mighty to save" (v. 17). God is present with His people. The exile in Babylon might be long, the punishment for their sin painful, but God will never forget His covenant of mercy and steadfast love. Through Zephaniah, God reveals His heart, His fatherly regard for His children.

- He will take great delight in you,
- He will quiet you with His love,
- He will rejoice over you with singing (v. 17).

It is time to celebrate God's love, and the Lord almighty invites and gathers His people for the festival.

Luke 1:39–55. Soon after the angel Gabriel's announcement, Mary visits Elizabeth, her relative, who is six months pregnant with her first child. The fact that both women are expecting is an occasion for rejoicing, as each son is destined for a special role in the redemption of Israel.

Mary travels to a village in Judea. At her greeting, the child in Elizabeth's womb stirs—leaps for joy—at the impulse of the Holy Spirit. Elizabeth, too, is filled with the Spirit. She understands that Mary's news marks the beginning of the fulfillment of God's promise to send the Messiah. Her relative is to be the mother of the Savior, the Lord. Elizabeth naturally blesses Mary, as she herself has been blessed by Mary's visit.

The hymn of praise that Mary sings—or speaks—is called the Magnificat (from the Latin "to glorify"). Her words are reminiscent of Old Testament psalms, but show an even closer connection to Hannah's song at the dedication of her son Samuel in the Lord's service (1 Samuel 2:1–10). Mary's hymn expresses joy in God's help and deliverance, once promised and now realized for Abraham's descendants. The Magnificat extols the greatness of God for His people. But Mary's adoration is profoundly personal: "The Mighty One has done great things for me" (v. 49; italics added). She praises God for her unique role in God's mighty act of salvation, indeed, for the gift of a son as her own Savior.

The hymn unfolds a major theme in Luke's gospel and in the Christian message: the overthrow of human ways and expectations (the "great reversal"). God reverses the ordinary "rules" of life by choosing the humble and lowly to achieve His purposes. In this way, "no one may boast before Him" (1 Corinthians 1:27–29).

For Mary, the great reversal means life for God's people. It also means a special place in the story of the Savior's birth. "All generations will call me blessed," she confesses, "for the Mighty One has done great things for me" (Luke 1:48–49).

Discussing the Text

1. Describe Zephaniah's message in terms of "bad" news (Law) and "good" news (Gospel).

2. What does Mary's hymn of praise express?

3. How does Mary's hymn of praise unfold the theme of the overthrow of human ways and expectations?

4. How do the words of Philippians 4:4–9 parallel the message of Mary's song of praise?

Connect

Even though God's ancient people deserved only judgment, God promised to redeem and restore the nation and He kept His promise. By itself, God's word of condemnation—revealed in the Law—leads only to despair. Humankind is "guilty as charged," with no right to appeal God's righteous verdict. In Christ, though, God's final word is "not guilty." He now delights in us and quiets us with His love, love revealed in His only Son. As God chose Mary, a humble, sinful servant, by His grace, He chooses us also through His love in Jesus our

Savior. By the Spirit's power, Mary responds to God's promise in faith. Believers today respond in praise and service to God's priceless gift of salvation.

In many respects, the world operates on the principles of merit: we are "rewarded" for our knowledge or efforts or skill or achievement. In sending His Son to earth, God reverses ordinary human ways to reveal His unmerited, undeserved goodness and love.

Christians, too, may fall prey to the lure of "self-justification" before God and others. The Gospel, however, proclaims pure grace. God forgives, not on the basis of merit or worthiness, but through Christ. In the Law we see both God's righteousness and our own flaws and failures. In the Gospel we see the Savior who redeems us with His blood and makes us His beloved, forgiven children—all by His mercy alone! Like Mary, we confess, "[The Lord] has done great things for me!"

1. How does God reverse ordinary human ways to reveal His unmerited, undeserved goodness and love for all people?

2. How is God's great reversal revealed in Jesus' death and resurrection? Consider: What do we receive because of Jesus' death on the cross and glorious resurrection?

3. God's great reversal is considered "foolishness" to those who have not received the gift of saving faith in Jesus. How might God's plan of salvation by grace alone through faith alone in Jesus alone seem foolish?

4. God's great reversal gives us life—eternal life. Because of God's great love for you and all people demonstrated in the life, death, and resurrection of Jesus, God declares us sinners, "Not guilty" through faith. Write a hymn of praise for that which God accomplished for you

by His great plan of reversal. Plan to share your hymn of praise during the closing worship.

Vision

To Do This Week

Family Connection

1. What would it be like if parents and children reversed roles for a day?

2. Discuss how God reversed roles with us when He sent Jesus (Jesus lived a perfect life and suffered and died for our sins).

3. How does Jesus' love for us change our lives?

Personal Reflection

1. Write the words from Philippians 4:4–9 on a note card. Place the card in a conspicuous place, where you will read it often.

2. Pray daily the hymn of praise you wrote.

3. Share God's great reversal with a friend or loved one this week.

Closing Worship

Share your hymn of praise as the closing worship activity.

For Next Week

Read Luke 2:1–20 in preparation for the next session.

Session 3

Jesus Is Born

(Luke 2:1–20)

Focus

Theme: Reconciled!

Law/Gospel Focus

All people are separated by their sinful nature from God and from one another. Through Jesus' death on the cross God has reconciled the world to Him. Through faith in Jesus Christ, God provides us the assurance of His mercy and eternal love and enables us to demonstrate His mercy and eternal love to others.

Objectives

By the power of the Holy Spirit working through God's Word we will

1. describe the events surrounding Jesus' birth and their significance;
2. affirm our human need and God's rich provision in His Son, Jesus, who was sent to earth to reconcile a world soaked in sin;
3. recommit ourselves to demonstrate God's mercy and eternal love to others.

Opening Worship

Sing or speak together one or more favorite Christmas carols/hymns.

Introduction

1. Describe the messages conveyed in the following headlines:
- Husband and Wife Reconcile after Year-Long Separation

- Father and Children Reconcile

- Two Friends Reconcile after Court Battle

2. Define the word reconcile.

3. On the following continuum indicate with an X how easy or difficult it is to reconcile differences. Be prepared to explain your answer.

Easy   Difficult

4. What differences might be easier to reconcile than others? Why?

In today's lesson we focus on that which is impossible for us to reconcile—our relationship with God. But God is able to do that which is impossible for us to accomplish. God sends His only Son into this world for one purpose—to reconcile sinners to Himself so that they might receive His forgiveness and eternal love.

Inform

Reading the Text

Before you read the familiar account of Jesus' birth, list as many of the events you can remember in the order in which they happened.

Now read aloud Luke 2:1–20.

Compare your list of the events surrounding the birth of Jesus with the actual events recorded in Luke's account.

The birth of the world's Redeemer takes places in the days of history's most famous ruler, Caesar Augustus. The first of Rome's emperors, Augustus governed the whole of the Mediterranean world from 27 B.C. until his death in A.D. 14. He decreed a census or "enrollment" of the empire to determine the population—and basis for tax revenue—of the various provinces and regions. The first enrollment was likely ordered in 8 B.C. The enrollment of Judah's towns and villages probably began around 6 B.C. Jesus, then, was born around 5 B.C.; Herod died in April, 4 B.C.

Luke mentions Quirinius as "governor of Syria" because the province of Syria, just north of Palestine, exercised limited control—mostly supervisory—over Herod's kingdom. The Roman Quirinius was governor in 6–4 B.C., and again in A.D. 6–9. The enrollment was taken of families according to their ancestral tribes. Those people who no longer resided in their "own town" were required to travel, at their personal expense, to register with Roman or local authorities. Because Joseph and Mary were from the tribe of Judah, and descendants of King David, they, too, were obligated to journey from Nazareth to Bethlehem, a distance of more than 70 miles. Bethlehem, birthplace and "home" of Israel's great ruler, was a small village south of Jerusalem.

Though brief and simple, Luke's description of Jesus' birth introduces the greatest event in human history. The Lord of lords and King of kings arrives quietly, modestly among His creation. The crowds in Bethlehem, in the frantic rush to register and return home, miss the mystery of Immanuel, "God with us." The humble circumstances—a feeding trough for a bed, an animal shelter—betray the majesty of the "Word become flesh." Yet the glory of Jesus' birth rests precisely in the hidden truth: the eternal Son of God enters our world as the servant of sinners, to die on the cross for the redemption of all God's people.

"Wrapped ... in cloths" refers to wrapping the baby in strips of cloth, a tight little bundle. Mary lay Jesus in a manger, a feeding trough in a stable or, as ancient Christians believed, a cave. God's gift to the world is silent, unimpressive in many ways. The honor of greeting the Savior is given to shepherds, humble men with a meaningful place in society and religious tradition. Shepherds watched flocks throughout the year. Most of their sheep were destined for sacrifice at the Jerusalem temple.

Many times in the past an "angel of the Lord" carried a divine message to humans. Here, too, on the most joyous of occasions, an "angel of the Lord" brings a glorious message. A Savior, who is Christ (Messiah) and Lord, is born in David's village. The word Lord (Kyrios in Greek) is often a translation of the Hebrew Yahweh in the Old Testament. The Greek word Christ (Messiah in Hebrew) means "Anointed One." The Savior in Bethlehem is thus true God, Yahweh, in human flesh.

Angel means "messenger." This messenger from God strikes terror in the shepherds' hearts. Moreover, the glory of the Lord, the heavenly radiance that marks God's presence, signals a remarkable event on earth. God's most profound revelation of His glory has taken place: the birth of His only Son, the Savior, "Christ the Lord."

Although the shepherds do not request a sign, the angel provides a striking portrait of the Savior's birth. The child sleeps in a manger, wrapped in simple clothing. Other angels join in the announcement. Like an ancient chorus in worship, the "great company" joins together in song to welcome the Lord of the universe. In biblical language as well as modern usage, "company of the heavenly host" has connotations of a vast army. Here, however, the army announces peace. "Glory to God" reflects God's mighty power and grace revealed in Jesus for the world. "In the highest" means among all the saints and angels of heaven. The first part of the angelic hymn, therefore, praises the majesty of God.

The second part of the hymn affirms that God's gift in Christ brings peace and well-being (the Old Testament "shalom"). "On earth" completes the circle of God's salvation—in heaven and on earth. Later, St. Paul would confess, "at the name of Jesus every knee should bow in heaven and on earth" (Philippians 2:10). "Peace" makes possible a relationship between God and humankind, and, rooted in God's forgiveness, relationships among His people. All people are separated by nature from God and from one another. Because Jesus has taken away our sins, God is reconciled to the world. Through faith in Christ we have assurance of God's mercy and eternal love.

Discussing the Text

1. What evidence does the text provide that God works in and

through everyday events in order to fulfill that which He has promised for years?

2. Why could the event described by Luke be considered the greatest event in human history?

3. How might we expect the King of kings and Lord of lords to arrive in this world? Compare your expectations to the humility in which God wraps this event.

4. Jesus enters the world more like a servant's child than a king. Why is this appropriate for Jesus? Consider Matthew 20:28 before you answer.

5. Why is the presence of angels not surprising at the birth of the Savior?

6. What is the significance of the "peace" the angels proclaim in their hymn of praise?

Connect

To a world torn by hostility and hardship, God sends the light of His salvation in the birth of a child, who is "Christ the Lord." Though people reject God's Word and "turn away" His truth—we have "no room" in our hearts—the Lord of grace and glory descends from heaven to bring us forgiveness, peace, and favor with God the Father.

God's righteousness and majesty frighten sinful men and women. In His Word God reveals His ways and will, and shows how far we fall short of His divine glory. The Good News is that God draws near in humility and love, born of a woman to redeem His people forever. Jesus is the eternal Son who displays the kind, compassionate face of the merciful Father. In His birth we witness, up close and intimately, God's love in action.

1. What is the significance of the Christmas account to you?

2. Sometimes because of the business of the season, we have "no room" for Jesus. Compare this "no room" to the message of the innkeeper to Mary and Joseph.

3. Describe in your own words the significance of God's plan of reconciliation to you.

4. Review the angels' hymn of praise. Write a prayer of praise for that which God has accomplished in your life through His Son's life, death, and resurrection. Be prepared to share the prayer during the closing-worship activity.

Vision

To Do This Week

Family Connection

1. Ask, "Why do we celebrate Christmas?"
2. Then ask, "How does our celebration reflect the reason we celebrate?"
3. Redefine reconcile.
4. How is reconciliation evident in our family?
5. How does Jesus' love for us empower us to reconcile even the most difficult conflict we may have?

Personal Reflection

1. Take time to reflect on the wonders God reveals in the birth of His Son, Jesus.
2. Praise God for the reconciliation He has provided you by His grace through faith in Jesus.
3. Share the real meaning of Christmas with a friend or loved one.

Closing Worship

Pray aloud the prayers of praise you wrote earlier.

For Next Week

Read Luke 2:41–52 in preparation for the next session.

Session 4

God Makes Us His Children

(Luke 2:41–52)

Focus

Theme: In My Father's House

Law/Gospel Focus

We often fail to worship God "in Spirit and truth." Jesus' death on the cross brings forgiveness to God's people and empowers them to be regular and faithful in "our Father's house." As we hear God's Word and receive His body and blood in the Sacrament we worship our Savior God.

Objectives

By the power of the Holy Spirit working through God's Word we will
1. explain the reason that Mary, Joseph, and Jesus went to Jerusalem;
2. describe the significance of Jesus' statement, "I had to be in My Father's house";
3. confess our failure to worship God "in Spirit and truth";
4. praise God for the forgiveness Jesus won for us on the cross and the power He provides to us so that we might be regular and faithful in worship.

Opening Worship

Sing or speak together "Lord, Open Now My Heart to Hear."

> Lord, open now my heart to hear,
> And through Your Word to me draw near;
> Preserve that Word in purity
> That I Your child and heir may be.

Your Word it is that heals my heart,
That makes me whole in ev'ry part;
Your Word of joy within me sings,
True peace and blessedness it brings.

To God the Father, God the Son,
To God the Spirit, three in one,
Honor and praise forever be
Now and through all eternity!

Introduction

1. What expectation do you have when people visit your home (e.g., take shoes off, watch children)?

2. What would you do if a person, couple, or family failed to live up to these expectations?

We often fail to live up to God's expectations when we visit His house.

3. How do we at times fail to live up to God's expectations when we visit His house?

Thanks be to God! He continues to invite us back to His house even when we fail to meet His expectations, and He offers us His forgiveness through the Gospel—the Good News of Jesus' death on the cross for our sins—provided by the proclaimed Word of God and the visible Word of God (sacraments) offered in worship. In this lesson we will witness Jesus in "His Father's house" and the significance of our being in "our Father's house" regularly and faithfully.

Inform

Reading the Text

Read aloud Luke 2:41–52.

Worship and instruction in God's Word. Both themes were vital to life in ancient Israel.

When a Jewish boy was still very young, his parents began his religious education with simple prayers and the memorization of Bible passages. The brief statement, "Hear O Israel: The LORD our God, the LORD is one" (Deuteronomy 6:4), provided a daily confession of faith and invocation in the home. Parents were called by God to "impress" the commandments and scriptural teachings upon their children at all stages of life and in a variety of settings. At age six, a child was traditionally sent to the synagogue school, where he learned God's Word and basic reading and writing skills. At age 13, he became a "son of the Commandment" (through the rite of bar mitzvah) and was obligated to attend the festivals.

The Old Testament describes three major annual feasts: (1) Unleavened Bread or Passover; (2) Weeks or Pentecost; and (3) Booths. These festivals, celebrated at different times of the year, were joyful occasions, marked by singing, music, dancing, special meals, and sacrifices. All adult male Israelites were required to attend the feasts at Jerusalem, the Lord's sanctuary. Women and children often accompanied their husbands and parents, and it was customary for extended families to travel together—for fellowship, for support, and for security.

Joseph and Mary were godly examples for Jesus, obedient to the Lord's Word and faithful every year in their observance of the Passover festival. They stayed the entire week—Passover lasted from sunset of the 14th day to the 21st day of the first month—and then prepared for the return trip to Nazareth. Because families traveled in large groups, parents may not have known precisely where their children were throughout the journey. In many cases, the caravan included pack animals, carts, and pets, sometimes stretching for miles along the roads and paths. Women with small children likely rode together, and men walked with older boys and the heavy wagons. Joseph and Mary may have assumed that Jesus was safe with the other children, or perhaps had entrusted the boy's care to a relative. Under such conditions, it was not uncommon for a child to remain "lost in the crowd" for a full day.

Jesus' parents, then, quickly return to Jerusalem—a one day journey back—and begin the search for their son. "After three days" likely refers to the total time from the family's first departure from Jerusalem. Joseph and Mary find Jesus in the temple courts, one of the numerous halls or porches surrounding the sanctuary, a traditional place for teaching. The young boy is a model student: He listens to the teachers, the experts in religious doctrine and life, and asks thoughtful, reverent questions. Jesus does not teach, He inquires, answers, and learns. Yet His knowledge of God's Word and His understanding of the ways and truths of Israel's faith "amazes" the teachers. (The nuance is "astonishment almost beyond belief.") Though true Son of God, Jesus, even as a youth, is humble, submissive to His Father's will. This is the only instance of Jesus listening in the presence of teachers. In the future, the Lord Himself will be the teacher and prophet to God's people.

Jesus' parents, too, are astonished. (The meaning here is "overwhelmed," "greatly astounded.") Mary's question betrays a sense of parental anguish and displeasure, because to this point Jesus has been the dutiful child. From a human perspective, His actions appear disrespectful, even disobedient. But to the eyes of faith Jesus obeys the call of His heavenly Father. His question, "Why were you searching for Me?," reveals that Mary and Joseph need to remember the true identity and mission of their son: He is the Son of God, the Savior of the world.

"I had to be in My Father's house" is the first public proclamation by Jesus of His unique relationship to God. It is also a statement of absolute devotion to His ministry. Jesus, David's royal Son, fully identifies with His Father's house, the temple, and reveals to His parents His earthly life's purpose: to offer Himself as the one, final sacrifice for the sins of the world.

Joseph and Mary do not understand Jesus' words. Only after the work of redemption was finished would Mary, the disciples, and the early Christians grasp the truth of Jesus' divine nature and mission.

Joseph, Mary, and Jesus return to Nazareth to live in peace and quiet until the appearance of John the Baptizer in the desert. (Joseph probably died before Jesus began His public ministry.) As Mary watched her son grow and mature, she "treasured" the memories of God's providence and goodness to Jesus, Son of Man and Son of God.

Discussing the Text

1. Explain the reason that Mary, Joseph, and Jesus went to Jerusalem. How does their obedience demonstrate their faith in God?

2. What was the significance of Jesus' response to His mother's question, "I had to be in My Father's house"?

3. What was the reason for Joseph and Mary's astonishment?

Connect

Jesus is obedient to the heavenly Father. His desire to remain at the temple, though a source of anxiety for His earthly parents, reveals His devotion to His Father's Word and will. For our part, we live as disobedient children. Since Adam and Eve, all people have been born in sin and therefore by nature reject God's Word and will. Jesus' perfect obedience, all the way to the cross, is, however, our hope for reconciliation with God. By His saving work Christ restores the relationship between God and His people. We are redeemed!

Though we often fail to worship God "in Spirit and in truth," Jesus brings forgiveness to God's people in His death and resurrection. He also empowers us to be regular and faithful in "our Father's house." By hearing God's Word and receiving His gifts in Baptism and Holy Communion we worship our Savior God. We respond, then, in praise, thanksgiving, witness, and service.

1. How do we fail to worship God "in Spirit and truth"?

2. What does God continue to offer to us in spite of our failures?

3. How does that which God provides to us—forgiveness for our failures through faith in Christ Jesus—empower us to be regular and faithful in worship?

4. What else does God through His Word empower us to do?

Vision

To Do This Week
Family Connection
1. Discuss why you attend worship as a family.
2. What blessing does God provide you in worship?
3. Why does God continue to invite us to His house even though we at times sin against Him and others?
4. Why is it important that your family set aside daily time for worship—Bible study, devotions, prayers?

Personal Reflection
1. Confess your failure to worship God "in Spirit and truth."
2. Praise God for the forgiveness He provides through faith in Christ Jesus for all of your failures.
3. Recommit yourself to be faithful and regular in worship.
4. Share with a friend and/or loved one the reason for your regular worship attendance.

Closing Worship
Pray together:
Heavenly Father, God of all grace, waken our hearts that we may

never forget Your blessings but steadfastly thank and praise You for all Your goodness, that we may live in Your fear until with all Your saints we praise You eternally in Your heavenly kingdom; through Jesus Christ, our Lord. Amen.

For Next Week

Read Matthew 6:25–34 and John 1:1–18 in preparation for the next session.

Session 5

God Takes Care of His Children

(Matthew 6:25–34; John 1:1–18)

— Focus —

Theme: Don't Worry!

Law/Gospel Focus

Worry is a mark of unbelief—a lack of trust in God's promise in Christ. We are all sinners and guilty of this lack of trust. In Christ, God has forgiven all our sins—above all our unbelief—and brought us into His kingdom of forgiveness and love. This forgiveness changes our priorities—from satisfying our own earthly needs first (we trust that God will provide for us) to putting others' needs first.

Objectives

By the power of the Holy Spirit working through God's Word we will
1. explain the theme of the Sermon on the Mount;
2. describe how worry is a mark of unbelief;
3. confess our lack of trust in God's promises and receive the assurance of Christ's complete forgiveness;
4. seek ways to meet the needs of others.

Opening Worship

Pray together the Lord's Prayer; then speak responsively the Fourth Petition of the Lord's Prayer and Luther's explanation.
All: Give us this day our daily bread.
Leader: What does this mean?
Participants: God certainly gives daily bread to everyone without our prayers, even to all evil people, but we pray in this petition that God would lead us to realize this, and to receive our daily bread with thanksgiving.

Leader: What is meant by daily bread?

Participants: Daily bread includes everything that has to do with the support and needs of the body, such as food, drink, clothing, shoes, house, home, land, animals, money, goods, a devout husband or wife, devout children, devout workers, devout and faithful rulers, good government, good weather, peace, health, self-control, good reputation, honor, good friends, faithful neighbors, and the like.

Introduction

Worry is something we all suffer from at one time or another. To stretch your understanding about worry, use the following exercise.

1. What comes to mind when you hear the word worry? List all the words and phrases that come to mind.

2. What cartoon character(s) come to mind when you examine your list of words concerning worry? Why?

Pick one cartoon character that best describes your list of words.

3. How does it feel to be that cartoon character? List as many "feeling" words as possible to describe the character.

4. Examine your list of "feeling" words. Identify any that seem to "fight against each other" (are opposites). Now select the two words that fight best against each other.

5. What plant comes to mind when you think about the two "feeling" words that fight against each other? Why? List as many plants as possible.

Now vote on the plant that best describes the two fighting words.

6. How is the plant you selected like worry? Write a sentence or two telling how the plant is like worry. Share comparisons.

This indirect teaching strategy called synectics helps participants to stretch their understanding of worry by using analogies.

In today's lesson we will examine worry—its cause and its effects in our lives. We will study what Jesus says about worry and ultimately come to the conclusion that it is a characteristic of our sinful nature. We will affirm the forgiveness Jesus won for all sin and be empowered by His love to trust more fully in His promises, including the promise to provide all we need to sustain this life.

Inform

Reading the Text

"Worry gives a small thing a big shadow."

Everyone has needs. Men and women, adults and children alike, all people live with daily cares and concerns. Water. Bread. Clothing. Shelter. For many today, these are the absolute "minimum requirements" of life. In ancient times, they were often rare treasures. "What will we eat? What will we drink? What will we wear?" At times, the small things in life cast a big shadow. Jesus directs His disciples to the true priority in God's kingdom.

The setting is the Sermon on the Mount. Jesus gathers His disciples—both His chosen followers and individuals from the "crowds"

(Matthew 4:25)—and begins to teach the "good news" of the kingdom of God. He speaks, as always, with authority; He reveals God's will for His people, a plan for living that flows from the heart of the heavenly Father. Gently and with patience, He confronts human beings with their many failures: disregard for God's Word, rebellion against His ways, apathy toward His gracious rule. At the same time, though, Jesus reveals the Father's love toward His fallen children. As God's Anointed, the Messiah, Jesus reveals God's kingdom in His own ministry. He is the Servant Savior, who brings righteousness and mercy and peace to God's people (5:6–8). He is the Light of the world, who scatters the darkness of sin and ignorance (5:14–16). He is the fulfillment of "the Law [and] Prophets" (5:17), whose words call sinners to repentance and guides forgiven sinners to know and seek His will. The Sermon on the Mount reveals that the kingdom of God focuses exclusively on Jesus, God's gracious gift to humankind. In Christ, God's people are new creations, called and strengthened to live as disciples.

Jesus' teaching is remarkably direct: "Do not worry" (6:25). In truth, most people of His day lived in constant anxiety and fear. Beside the usual concerns of day-to-day existence, ordinary men and women dealt with sickness and diseases, violence and intimidation. The wealthy often oppressed the poor, the vast majority of the population. Local officials frequently imposed harsh judgments upon families and communities. Bandits regularly roamed the countryside, waiting to rob and kill travelers (see for example, Luke 10:30). Life was, in many respects, "nasty, brutish, and short." From a human perspective, it was only natural, perhaps even wise, to worry about everything.

Yet Jesus reveals that worry—the word means to harbor a steady anxiety toward the future—is rooted in faithlessness. To worry about tomorrow's needs and concerns, that is, what to eat, drink or wear, is to show a lack of trust in God, the Creator and Provider of all life. As illustrations of genuine dependence upon God, Jesus points to the simple truths of God's creation. Birds do not anxiously labor to plant, harvest, and store their daily food. The gracious heavenly Father, however, provides for all their needs (v. 26). In a similar way, the "lilies of the field" blossom and flourish in beauty beyond comparison, all as a result of God's creative power and lavish grace toward the earth (vv. 28–29). All too quickly, though, these wildflowers are destined for destruction, "thrown into the fire" as fuel or everyday refuse. In both examples, Jesus draws on the common practice of teaching from "the lesser to the greater." If God shows such concern for "mere" birds and flowers, how much more is He intimately concerned for human beings, made in His image and likeness!

Jesus' point is clear: worry adds nothing good to life, especially not length or quality of days. Instead, regular and even occasional worry convicts all people as individuals of "little faith" (v. 30). To worry about food and drink and clothing is a denial of God's promise: it is to live as "pagans," that is, as apart from a covenant relationship with God, in unbelief and unrepentant sin (v. 32).

In truth, Jesus affirms, the heavenly Father knows His creatures' needs. According to His good and gracious will, He desires to bestow His many blessings on humanity, the blessings that nourish, support, and protect physical life. But above all, God desires His people to "seek first His kingdom and His righteousness" (v 33). The kingdom is God's rule in and among His people, revealed now in its fullness in Jesus. Kingdom-living centers on God's Messiah, who brings God's gifts of forgiveness and life to unrighteous people. In Christ, God freely gives His righteousness to everyone who trusts in Him. To seek the heavenly Father's kingdom and righteousness, then, is to look to Jesus in repentance, in faith, in confidence of God's mercy and blessing. With their eternal salvation secure, God's people trust Him to provide the basics of life—"all these things" (v. 33)—as well.

Discussing the Text

1. What is the setting for Jesus' teaching about worry? What is the significance of this setting?

2. How does Jesus reveal God's kingdom in His ministry?

3. People who read the Sermon on the Mount might be left with a feeling of impossibility. Ultimately, it is impossible to do that which

Jesus commands. What does Jesus' teachings in the Sermon on the Mount tell us about our need for a Savior?

4. What is the root of worry? What is the opposite of worry?

5. What does Jesus affirm in His teachings about worry?

6. How does the fact that Jesus is the Word of God in the flesh give us comfort?

Connect

Worry is an indication of our sinful nature, a lack of trust in God's gracious promise in Christ. Yet all believers worry, even children. Young people have many fears and anxieties, from violence on the street to abuse and neglect at home. The sad reality is that our world is irreparably damaged by sin and evil. And we, too, of course, are part of the problem. We doubt God's promises, and therefore we hurt or ignore our neighbor. We are sinners, guilty of breaking faith with God. In Christ, though, God has forgiven our sin—above all our unbelief—and brought us into His kingdom of forgiveness and love. In His mercy He has redeemed us from the power of sin and Satan. Though we still worry and doubt, we have Christ's sure promise to forgive us and renew us daily by His grace.

Forgiveness in Christ changes our priorities. While unbelievers seek exclusively to satisfy earthly needs (at times we too fall prey to our selfish ambitions and demands), God's people have a different purpose and direction in life. We know our heavenly Father will take care of us. He has given us life and salvation, and will equip us to share His Good News in the world. Justified by faith, we serve God by seeking to help all others in need, especially our fellow believers. We endure the hardships of life, assured of His promise to work everything for our good.

1. What does the fact that all people worry tell us about the spiritual condition of the world?

2. Despite our faithlessness what does God continue to provide for us?

3. How does forgiveness change our priorities?

4. Identify a person who reflects the forgiveness of Jesus in her/his priorities. How does this person reflect God's love in Christ?

5. Write a prayer of thanksgiving to God for providing for all of your needs, including the greatest need of all—forgiveness of sins. Be prepared to share the prayer during closing worship.

Vision

To Do This Week

Family Connection

1. Confess to one another worries you have.

2. How does our worrying demonstrate a lack of trust in God, who provides for all of our needs? Assure one another of God's forgiveness through Jesus.

3. Determine to share the statement "God promises to provide" with a family member who worries.

Personal Reflection

1. List all of the things about which you worry.

2. Draw a cross over the list to remind you of the forgiveness Jesus won for you that empowers you to "trust in God above all things."

3. Share with a friend or loved one the confidence God provides you through faith in Jesus.

Closing Worship

Pray the prayers of thanksgiving written earlier.

For Next Week

Read Luke 3:15–17, 21–22 and Matthew 11:1–19; 14:1–12 in preparation for the next session.

Session 6

John Tells about Jesus

(Luke 3:15–17, 21–22; Matthew 11:1–19; 14:1–12)

Focus

Theme: Not Guilty Only Through Christ

Law/Gospel Focus

All people stand under God's wrath and therefore His judgment because of sin. We have absolutely no claim before God; we have only guilt. But the Good News of the Messiah brings us life and salvation. Jesus is the "Powerful One," who defeated sin, death, and hell in His death and resurrection. Through Baptism into Christ we are forgiven and made new creatures, ready and able to serve our Savior.

Objectives

By the power of the Holy Spirit working through God's Word we will
1. identify the significance of John's question about Jesus and John's bold confession of Jesus as the Messiah;
2. confess our sinful state and cling in faith to the "not guilty" verdict won by Jesus through His death on the cross;
3. seek new opportunities to serve Jesus.

Opening Worship

Sing or speak together stanzas 1 and 2 of "On Jordan's Bank the Baptist's Cry."

On Jordan's bank the Baptist's cry
Announces that the Lord is nigh;
Awake and hearken, for he brings
Glad tidings of the King of kings!

> Then cleansed be ev'ry life from sin;
> Make straight the way for God within,
> And let us all our hearts prepare
> For Christ to come and enter there.

Introduction

The jury read the verdict, "Guilty!" Afterward the judge sentenced the convicted criminal to death. Just before the criminal was escorted to his cell to await execution a victim of the criminal stood up and shouted, "No! Let this man live. I will take the punishment pronounced by the court!"

Sound bizarre? Even impossible? Of course this would never happen in real life! But it has!

1. Read Romans 5:6–11. How are the events described by Paul much like the story?

2. Describe what God has done for you in your own words. Then share what you wrote with a partner.

In today's lesson we will experience John's cry for repentance and the assurance only Jesus can give for the forgiveness of sins and eternal life. Jesus declares us "not guilty" through His life, death, and resurrection.

Inform

Reading the Text

Read aloud Luke 3:15–17, 21–22 and Matthew 11:1–19; 14:1–12.
Luke 3:15–17, 21–22. Is John the Christ? His appearance in the

desert, preaching and baptizing for the forgiveness of sins, captured the imagination of many people. The nation awaited God's Messiah. Israel looked forward, with great expectation, to the Lord's coming, the day of deliverance, the day of God's judgment upon His enemies and salvation for His people. John certainly proclaimed judgment. Like an ax upon the root of a tree, God's Law was ready to "cut down" sinners, to destroy the wicked in the flames of eternal punishment (Luke 3:9).

But John's message was not simply directed to Gentiles and tax collectors and soldiers. He spoke to all people. No one can escape the righteous judgment of God. In the light of the divine Law, everyone is guilty—John the Baptizer, too. The prophet is only a witness, a messenger, who baptizes fellow sinners with water for the forgiveness of sin. His task is to prepare for the Messiah, who alone has the power to save and restore God's fallen children. John is a lowly servant, so lowly in fact that he is not "worthy to untie" the Savior's sandals (Luke 3:16).

"He will baptize you with the Holy Spirit and with fire." John's mission is temporary; his baptism points toward the final, complete washing and renewal that the Messiah pours out on His disciples. Baptized into Jesus' death and resurrection, God's people receive the gift of the Holy Spirit; they are born from above of water and the Spirit (John 3:3, 5).

"Jesus was baptized too" (Luke 3:21). The Lord's public ministry begins in Jordan's waters. Luke describes only the highlights—the baptism, the open heaven, the Spirit's descent "in bodily form like a dove" (v. 22). The climax comes in the voice of the Father: "You are My Son, whom I love; with You I am well pleased" (v. 22). In Jesus' baptism, the triune God is revealed: Father, Son, and Holy Spirit.

The gospel of Matthew provides the context and significance of Jesus' baptism. As the Son of God, Jesus was sinless as He stood in the Jordan River. Why, then, does He submit to baptism by John? Jesus identifies Himself with His fallen creation. The Savior of the world declares His solidarity, His unity and fellowship, with sinful men and women. The Savior serves those He comes to save. In the first of many displays of humility and selfless ministry, Jesus offers Himself for His beloved people, to "fulfill" their needs with His rich supply of grace and strength.

Matthew 11:1–19. While in prison, John the Baptizer heard the various reports about Jesus' extraordinary ministry: "He preaches with conviction." "He teaches with authority." "He heals the sick and casts out demons." Like many others, John was waiting for the revelation of God's saving power in the Messiah. When Jesus appeared, John testified, "This is the Son of God" (John 1:34). He pointed his own disciples to "the Lamb of God, who takes away the sin of the world" (John 1:29, 36). He even witnessed the gift of the Spirit and the heavenly Father's approval at Jesus' baptism.

But in prison, John was isolated. He was likely concerned about the delay of the kingdom. He wondered why God had not come with power to judge the world and ransom His captive people. Perhaps he heard stories of disillusionment, even resentment at Jesus' mission: "He welcomes sinners!" "He dines with tax collectors and prostitutes!" "He offers forgiveness and compassion to everyone!" Many people did not believe in or follow Jesus. Others were offended by His words and actions; some abandoned Him (John 6:66). John the Baptizer and his disciples wanted assurance that Jesus was, indeed, the Messiah, the Son of God.

In response, Jesus assures John with the promises of God's Word.

As Messiah, Jesus fulfills the Scriptures: He is the Servant of the Lord, the Savior whose mission was foretold by the prophet Isaiah (35:5–6; 61:1–3). God's work of salvation, His healing, forgiving, life-restoring salvation, was unfolding here and now among His people. It was a special blessing to see and believe the Son of God in person.

Jesus' questions to the crowd are rhetorical; He expects, of course, a definite "No!" John the Baptizer was an unwavering, determined prophet of God. No human opinion or influence distracted him from his ministry. He was not "a reed swayed by the wind" (v. 7). In the ancient world, bending reeds were proverbial (1 Kings 14:14–16), a sign of a frail and unsteady personality. John also set aside all earthly comforts and luxuries. He wore rough camel hair garments as a visual symbol of his vigorous call to repentance in the light of divine judgment. Like God's prophets in the past, John was not a puppet of the royal family, under the coercion and control of a king or queen. He spoke God's Word alone, and answered only to the almighty King of the universe.

John the Baptizer is, in fact, the messenger-prophet promised by God through Malachi (Matthew 11:11 and see Malachi 3:1). He is the new Elijah, sent to call people to a change of heart and life. He is a messenger to announce the arrival of the true Messiah.

Jesus, in turn, praises John. John is "great," not because of his character, but because of his call as the forerunner of the Messiah. John is still mortal. His work only prepares the way for God's work of salvation. When the work is finished (through the death of the Messiah for the sins of the world), John will take his place in the kingdom with the rest of God's people: simply as a redeemed sinner.

Jesus' comparison is a parable, appropriate for every individual and all people who reject the proclamation of the Good News. Like two groups of children who reproach each other for not "playing" properly, "this generation" does not know what it wants and is dissatisfied with whatever it is offered (vv. 16–17). John was too stern; Jesus is too tolerant. John preached repentance and judgment; Jesus welcomes humble sinners and freely forgives. John did not eat bread or drink wine; Jesus eats and drinks and even takes part in festival banquets.

Who is right? Both! God judges, but also forgives repentant sinners. God's people mourn for their sin, but also rejoice in faith over God's mercy. The threat of the Law gives way to the comfort of the Good News. God's wisdom in sending the Messenger and the Messiah is "proved right" in the growth of the kingdom, the salvation of His people (v. 19).

Matthew 14:1–12. John's life comes to a violent end. King Herod makes a rash promise to his wife's daughter, who requests the Baptizer's head on a platter (v. 8). John is executed; his disciples give him an honorable burial. Jesus mourns his death (14:13).

Discussing the Text

1. What is the essence of John's message?

2. How is John's ministry different from Jesus' ministry?

3. What is the significance of Jesus' baptism?

4. Why did John the Baptizer want assurance that Jesus was the Messiah, the Son of God?

5. How is John "great"?

Connect

God's Law applies to everyone. For John, no one was excluded from the call to repent and bring forth the fruit of repentance (Luke 3:8). All human beings stand under God's wrath, and therefore His judgment. We have absolutely no claim before God; we have only guilt. But the Good News the Messiah brings is life and salvation. Jesus is the "Powerful One," who defeats sin, death and hell in His death and resurrection. Through Baptism into Christ we are forgiven and made new creatures, ready and able to serve our Savior God.

Like people of every place and time, John wanted assurance. He and his disciples were seeking the certain truth that Jesus indeed is the Messiah sent by God. Jesus directs John to God's Word, the divine promises spoken first by the ancient prophets and written down in the Sacred Scriptures. For believers, the Bible testifies to Jesus. His ministry, suffering, sacrificial death, and resurrection all fulfill God's plan revealed in the Scriptures. We find our assurance of God's love and forgiveness in His Word of truth, which makes us "wise for salvation through faith in Christ Jesus" (2 Timothy 3:15).

1. To whom does God's Law apply? What is the significance of this fact?

2. What do we receive through Holy Baptism?

3. We too need the constant assurance of God's love and forgiveness. How does God provide assurance today?

4. What does God's assurance of His love in Christ motivate us to do?

5. Write a prayer of thanksgiving for the "not guilty" verdict God provided to us through His Son's death on the cross.

Vision

To Do This Week
Family Connection

1. Say, "God has declared us 'not guilty' through His Son's death on the cross." Let each family member share what this means to her/him.

2. Discuss each family member's Baptism. Then review the events that occurred on each of those days.

3. Compare what occurred at Jesus' baptism with your Baptism.

Personal Reflection

1. Reread Romans 5:7–11. Spend time meditating on God's great love for us.

2. Consider ways in which you can serve your God and Savior.

3. Take time to tell a friend or loved one of the "not guilty" verdict rendered for you through God's grace through faith in Jesus.

Closing Worship

Pray the prayers of thanksgiving written earlier.

For Next Week

Read John 2:1–11 in preparation for the next session.

Session 7

Jesus Changes Water into Wine

(John 2:1–11)

Focus

Theme: Prove It!

Law/Gospel Focus

We live in a world that demands proof. Because of sin, we doubt one another, and above all we doubt God. Yet Jesus condescends to sinful, unbelieving people to reveal His glory through miraculous signs. The greatest display of His glory is in the cross, where He took our stubborn pride and rebellion so that we might receive forgiveness. Jesus continues to reveal His glory in ordinary gifts—water, wine, and bread to pour out His grace—forgiveness and life. Through His gifts Jesus brings us true joy and reason to celebrate.

Objectives

By the power of the Holy Spirit working through God's Word we will

1. confess our doubts against God and rejoice in the forgiveness Jesus won for us on the cross;
2. affirm Jesus' presence and glory revealed in ordinary means—water, wine, and bread;
3. celebrate with joy the gifts God so graciously provides us through Jesus.

Opening Worship

Pray together:

Almighty, everlasting God, whose Son has assured forgiveness of sin and deliverance from eternal death, strengthen us by Your Holy Spirit that our faith in Christ increase daily, and we hold fast the hope that we shall not die but fall asleep and on

the Last Day be raised to eternal life; through Jesus Christ, our
Lord. Amen.

Introduction

"Prove it!"

1. In what situations have you or someone you know spoken these
words?

2. What causes us or others to speak these words?

In today's lesson we will witness the first of Jesus' miraculous signs
recorded in John's gospel. In this and subsequent signs Jesus reveals
His glory to sinful people. We will also see that Jesus revealed His
ultimate sign of glory on the cross and continues to reveal Himself
today to sinful people through His means of grace—Word and Sacraments—as proof of His everlasting love.

Inform

Reading the Text

The gospel of John portrays seven of Jesus' miraculous "signs"
from His public ministry. It is, to be sure, only a small sample of His
many miracles (see John 20:30; 21:25), but each story has special significance. The signs proclaim that God's kingdom and gracious rule
are a present reality in Jesus. Through each miracle, Jesus displays
His eternal glory, calls His disciples and the crowds to faith, and
strengthens faith in His self-revelation as the Lord and Savior of the
world. All seven signs in John's gospel disclose a unique truth about

the person and the work of the Messiah. (The seven miraculous signs are reported in 2:1–11; 4:46–54; 5:1–9; 6:5–13; 6:19–21; 9:1–7; 11:1–44.)

After His baptism by John in the Jordan River, Jesus begins to choose His own followers, His disciples. He chooses and calls ordinary people; the first six disciples were likely all fishermen. Andrew and an unnamed partner—perhaps John, the "disciple whom Jesus loved" (John 13:23), who wrote the gospel—leave the Baptizer immediately and completely to follow Jesus (John 1:39). Andrew brings his brother Simon to Jesus (1:40); John's brother James also becomes a disciple (Mark 1:16–20). Jesus then departs from Judea and travels north to Galilee. He calls Philip, who, like Andrew before him, shares his "discovery" with a close friend, Nathanael (John 1:45). "On the third day" (John 2:1), that is, from Nathanael's call, Jesus and His disciples—at this time, probably, Andrew and Peter, James and John, Philip and Nathanael—depart for Cana in Galilee to begin their ministry together.

The first major public event is a wedding. In ancient Israel, weddings usually began with a procession from the bride's home to the groom's home. (The ceremony took place up to a year after a formal betrothal; marriage contracts, often drawn up by parents while the couple was still young, included payment of the "price for the bride" to the woman's father; see Genesis 34:12.) After the blessing, the families shared a wedding dinner. The celebration, a joyful event with singing, dancing, and music, lasted for days, at times, a full week or more (see Judges 14:12).

"Jesus' mother" is present at the wedding dinner (2:1). Throughout the gospel of John, Mary, the mother of Jesus, remains anonymous; she is not mentioned by name. In ancient times, the title "mother of …" was a sign of deep respect toward both God and the family. Children were God's gifts to parents (see Psalm 127:3–5; Proverbs 31:28–30). To give birth to and raise godly sons and daughters was a mother's special joy and honor. As "Jesus' mother," Mary was held in high esteem by her family and friends. She will feel a mother's deep pain and sense of loss at the crucifixion of her Son (see John 19:25–27).

"They have no more wine" (2:3). The situation is an embarrassment, not simply to the parents and wedding couple, but to the entire family gathered for the celebration. Hospitality was an important social value in ancient communities. Hosts were expected, even obligated, to provide for guests, both friends and strangers. To refuse hospitality, or to run out of food and drink, was to risk public disgrace.

Mary's statement is actually a request. Jesus' reply, in fact, is more than an answer: it is an affirmation of His mission and destiny. "Dear woman" is a typical greeting of the day. Jesus does not intend any disrespect, rebuke, or lack of affection. It is, rather, His usual way of addressing women (see Matthew 15:28; Luke 13:12; John 4:21; 8:10; 19:26; 20:13). "Why do you involve me?" inquires into motives and assumptions. Mary knows Jesus' unique identity as God's Son, the promised Messiah. Does she understand, however, the true nature of His mission on earth? Is Jesus simply a new provider for God's people, a new Moses to provide manna and quail in the desert? "My time has not yet come" proclaims the hidden truth of Jesus' ministry, a ministry that focuses upon the "day" of suffering and death for the sins of the world.

Without a doubt, Mary knows that Jesus is able to provide for the banquet; she also trusts that He will provide, a sign of His grace and goodness toward the world.

"Six stone water jars" dramatize the magnitude of Jesus' act: the total volume of water was perhaps 180 gallons (v. 6). The jars had previously been used for "ceremonial washing," that is, for ritual and hygienic purposes. In the course of a day, men, women and children would become "unclean" through contact with dead animals, corpses, bodily fluids, foreigners, or forbidden foods. While unclean, a person was not permitted to engage in certain religious practices. All pious Jews who attended the wedding feast would have washed prior to eating and drinking. Without wine, however, the festival atmosphere was diminished, as well as the sacred character of the celebration. (A wedding feast is, in a sense, a celebration of God's goodness in marriage, just as marriage itself is a picture of God's covenant love toward His people.) At Jesus' word, though, the jars will no longer hold water to remove impurity; the jars will hold wine, a symbol of God's kindness and rich provision toward His joyful people (see Isaiah 25:6–8).

The servants obey Jesus completely and without delay (v. 7). At His instruction, they take the "new wine" to the "master of the banquet" (vv. 8, 9), probably the head waiter or a family friend chosen to manage the dinner and festivities. Though he does not know the source of the servant's supply, the master unwittingly states the key point to the bridegroom: the new is better than the old! Yet it is not the bridegroom who provides the finest wine, but the Messiah, the

Son of God. His appearance on earth signals a new day, a new life. The old ways, including the day of mourning and grief, are past. The true wedding celebration has begun! (See also John 3:27–29; Luke 5:33–35.)

"Revealed His glory" (John 2:11) does not mean the complete and final manifestation of His glory. Only suffering, death, resurrection and return to the Father reveals the full majesty of God's Son. Yet in the miraculous sign at Cana the disciples see a glimpse of His saving work. Later, too, as they reflected on the many events of His public ministry, the disciples came to understand their Lord and Savior as the fulfillment of all God's ancient promises.

Discussing the Text

1. What is the significance of Jesus' miraculous signs?

2. Why was running out of wine an embarrassment?

3. What is the significance of Jesus' statement "My time has not yet come"? When would Jesus' time come?

4. Jesus "revealed His glory" at the wedding. How did Jesus reveal His glory at the wedding? When did Jesus reveal His complete and final manifestation of glory?

Connect

We live in a world that demands proof. Human beings want evidence, some type of "demonstration" that backs up the claims of manufacturers, salespersons, educators, even politicians. Our lives are characterized by skepticism, distrust, cynicism. We are people who doubt one another, and above all we are people who doubt God. This lack of trust is sin. God's Law confronts us with our unbelief, our unwillingness to "fear, love, and trust God above all things." Yet Jesus condescends to sinful, unbelieving individuals to reveal His glory through His miraculous signs. The premier display of His glory is in the cross, where He takes to Himself our stubborn pride and rebellion. In His death and resurrection, we see God's love fully and freely demonstrated for our life.

In the midst of human need and apprehension, Jesus comes with His good gifts. His presence brings joy and true celebration. He uses ordinary gifts, water, wine, and bread (see John 6:1–13, 25–58) to pour out His grace—forgiveness and life. In Baptism, in the Lord's Supper, we are made new and renewed to follow the Savior.

1. What evidence can you provide that we live in a world that demands proof?

2. What proof did Jesus provide of the Father's love for us and all people?

3. God continues to use ordinary gifts. What ordinary gifts does God use today? What does God provide to us through these ordinary gifts?

4. Write a prayer of thanksgiving for God revealing His glory in the person and work of Jesus. Also, give thanks to God for continuing to

pour out His grace to us today through ordinary means—water, wine, and bread.

Vision

To Do This Week

Family Connection

1. Discuss the statement, "Prove it." What does it tell you about the person who says it? about the person or persons it is said to?

2. How did Jesus prove He was God's only Son?

3. What might you say to a person who tells you to prove it when you tell her/him of Jesus' love?

4. How can you prove your love to the members of your family? your friends? your enemies?

Personal Reflection

1. Confess your sinful doubts about others and God.

2. Rejoice in the forgiveness Jesus won for you from sinful doubts.

3. Spend time reading God's Word this week. Marvel at the glory of God revealed to us through His Word.

4. Share the love that God has revealed to your through Jesus' life, death, and resurrection with a friend or loved one.

Closing Worship

Pray together the prayers of thanksgiving written earlier in this session.

For Next Week

Read Luke 10:38–42 in preparation for the next session.

Session 8

Jesus Teaches Mary and Martha

(Luke 10:38–42)

Focus

Theme: In the Midst of Busy-ness

Law/Gospel Focus

Our daily problems and concerns can master us. We can become self-centered and selfish, preoccupied with this commitment or that obligation to the neglect of our spiritual life. Jesus continues to call us through His Word to the "the one thing needful." Through opportunities to hear His Word—worship, Bible study, Bible reading, devotions—we learn of God's will and our failure, we hear of His Good News of forgiveness through faith in Jesus, who died for all of our sin. Through His Word the Holy Spirit works to strengthen our faith so that we might follow Christ in our everyday experiences.

Objectives

By the power of the Holy Spirit working through God's Word we will
1. confess our neglect of spiritual matters as we become preoccupied with issues we face daily in our lives;
2. affirm Jesus' continued call to repentance through His Word so that we might receive the forgiveness won for us on the cross;
3. face everyday life experiences with a zeal and commitment to keep Jesus first in our lives.

Opening Worship

Sing or speak together "Lord, Keep Us Steadfast in Your Word."

Lord, keep us steadfast in Your Word;
Curb those who by deceit or sword
Would wrest the kingdom from Your Son
And bring to nought all He has done.

Lord Jesus Christ, Your pow'r make known,
For You are Lord of lords alone;
Defend Your holy Church that we
May sing Your praise triumphantly.

O Comforter of priceless worth,
Send peace and unity on earth;
Support us in our final strife
And lead us out of death to life.

Introduction

1. How busy is your life? Use the continuum to indicate your busy-ness with an X. Be prepared to explain why you placed the X where you did.

Calm   Busy

2. There are only 24 hours in a day. What things get squeezed out of your life? What is the danger of squeezing opportunities to hear God's Word out of your life?

In today's lesson we will see how even the most faithful of Jesus' followers can become preoccupied by the busy-ness life can bring—even to the neglect of that which is the one thing "needful" (KJV). But Jesus continues to invite us through His Word to hear of that which He has accomplished for our eternal welfare—namely, the forgiveness of sins and eternal life He won for us on the cross.

Inform

Reading the Text

Read aloud Luke 10:38–42.

"Only one thing is needed" (Luke 10:42). In the midst of numerous daily obligations—to self, to family, to work and friends—Jesus directs His followers to the one critical, urgent need: to hear His Word.

Jesus and the disciples are "on their way" (v. 38), walking the dusty roads of Galilee, Samaria, and Judea, preaching and teaching the Good News of the kingdom in every village. The gospel of Luke includes a major "travel narrative" (9:51–19:27), an extensive report on the final part of Jesus' public ministry before His arrival in Jerusalem, the holy city. During their travels, Jesus and the disciples, especially His apostles, were often guests in the homes of people who accepted His message and supported His mission. On one occasion they stayed in Bethany, where Martha and Mary welcomed the Lord willingly and with genuine hospitality. (For a second example of Mary and Martha's love and gratitude toward Jesus, see John 12:1–8.)

As an expression of hospitality, ancient peoples often prepared elaborate dinners for their guests. A meal was, in many respects, a symbol of the bond of friendship, trust, and mutual admiration among all gathered at the table. It was also an opportunity to show honor to distinguished persons. Hosts had certain obligations. A banquet celebration usually meant the best of meats (for example, the "fattened calf," Luke 15:23), the finest wines, and an assortment of vegetables and side dishes. In wealthy homes, servants garnered and cooked the food. The host, however, generally gave the orders and supervised the activity in the kitchen and elsewhere.

Mary "sat at the Lord's feet listening to what He said" (v. 39). Jesus often taught in the homes He visited or stayed in during His ministry (Luke 5:29–39; 7:36–50). In ancient Israel, a teacher sat in a prominent place while students gathered nearby on the floor or ground. Mary sits close to Jesus, probably right beside Him. She is captivated by His words and is, at least for the moment, oblivious to her household duties. She listens to Good News of God's salvation in the Messiah, Good News that calls all people to "seek first His kingdom and His righteousness" (Matthew 6:33; Luke 12:31).

Martha, on the other hand, is "distracted by all the preparations" (Luke 10:40). Perhaps Jesus' visit had been unexpected; perhaps the number of His followers put a strain on the provisions at hand. Perhaps Martha was the older sister, older than her brother Lazarus, too, and thus she feels responsible for arranging the dinner. She comes to Jesus in a moment of impatience and irritation. Her rebuke is really addressed to Mary, but she targets Jesus, too, for His apparent lack of concern. The issue is not that Mary started to help and then sat down to casually listen to the Master's teaching. Martha has been working by herself (v. 40). In her mind only one solution is possible: "Tell her to help me!" (v. 40).

Jesus, in turn, addresses Martha in a gentle, but direct, tone. The repetition of her name, "Martha, Martha" (v. 41), demonstrates His affection and concern for her welfare, but also the seriousness of His response. Martha is wrongly "worried." She is anxious about the details of life, details that in the light of the Kingdom have little or no ultimate significance. Today is the day of salvation; now is the time to receive God's gifts with quietness of heart and single-minded devotion. Martha is also "upset." She is angry over the course of events. She resents her sister's choice and wants Jesus to correct the wrong. But in fact the solution is not to take Mary away from the Good News, but to bring the Good News to Martha.

"Many things" are the what, when, where, how, and who of the dinner. Jesus simply reminds Martha, "only one thing is needed" (v. 42). An elaborate meal is not necessary. A few portions, perhaps only one, would have been sufficient. The "one thing" is to listen to Jesus and receive His words of life and forgiveness.

Martin Luther notes:

> It is better to omit everything but the Word. Nothing deserves to be fostered more than the Word; for the entire Scripture shows that this is to be in common use among Christians, and Christ Himself says (Luke 10:42) that one thing is needful: that Mary sit at the feet of Christ and hear His Word daily. This is the best part that is to be chosen, and it will never be taken away. It is an eternal Word. All the rest must pass away, no matter how much work it gives Martha to do. (What Luther Says, 884)

> (From What Luther Says, vol. 1, compiled by Ewald M. Plass. Copyright © 1959 by Concordia Publishing House. All rights reserved.)

Discussing the Text

1. Considering the culture, why is it not surprising that Martha is taking such drastic measures to demonstrate hospitality?

2. How does Jesus address Martha in a gentle way? What does this demonstrate?

3. What is the significance of Jesus statement, "only one thing is needed"?

Connect

How quickly daily problems and concerns can master us! We become self-centered and selfish, preoccupied with this commitment or that obligation to the utter neglect of our spiritual life. We ignore God's Word. We are too busy to attend worship. Our lives become built upon the shifting sands of work or recreation or simply "getting by." Jesus knows our weaknesses. He offers His forgiveness for the many times we have chosen to pursue our interests and ambitions rather than to follow Him. He calls us to repentance, lifts us up with His Word of mercy and encouragement, and anchors us firmly on the bedrock truth of God's kingdom, the hope of salvation in His atoning death and resurrection from the dead.

Jesus' Word is, however, urgent. Our tendency is to procrastinate, to put off our deep spiritual needs in the tumult of the day. Christians, too, are prone to find any and every excuse not to read or meditate on the Scriptures, even though God speaks to us and strengthens our faith through His Word. Jesus calls us to "the one thing needful." Whether we gather in weekly worship with our fellow believers or sit quietly in a chair with His promises, Christ is present with us. Through the Word, we learn of God's will and of our failures, we hear His Good News of forgiveness, and we are strengthened to follow Christ in our everyday responsibilities.

1. What issues in your life have a tendency to master you?

2. How can focusing your attention on these items alone hinder you participating in the "one thing ... needed"?

3. What comfort is there in knowing that Jesus understands our weakness?

4. What does Jesus invite "busy" Christians to do? What does He provide? Read Jesus' invitation in Matthew 11:28–30.

5. How can spending time in God's Word provide us help as we face daily living?

Vision

To Do This Week

Family Connection

1. Discuss how the busy-ness of your lives can or have become a distraction in your relationship to God? your relationship with one another?

2. Seek new ways in which your family can spend additional time in the "one thing ... needed"—God's Word—the most important thing in your lives.

Personal Reflection

1. When things become rough this week, spend some time in God's Word.

2. Make a commitment to study God's Word daily.

3. Pray that the Lord would strengthen your commitment to His Word.

4. Share Matthew 11:28–30 with a friend or loved one struggling with issues in his or her life.

Closing Worship

Sing or speak together "God's Word Is Our Great Heritage."

God's Word is our great heritage
And shall be ours forever;
To spread its light from age to age
Shall be our chief endeavor.
Through life it guides our way,
In death it is our stay.
Lord, grant, while worlds endure,
We keep its teachings pure
Throughout all generations.

For Next Week

Read Luke 4:14–32 in preparation for the next session.

Jesus Teaches in the Synagogue

(Luke 4:14–32)

Focus

Theme: Rejected!

Law/Gospel Focus

Because of sin people continue to reject God's Word. They reject His Law by continuing to wantonly and openly sin, to blame others for their sin, to fail to take responsibility for their sin, and to criticize His Law as no longer applicable for life today. As people reject God's Law, they in turn reject His Gospel—the Good News of forgiveness and eternal life Jesus won for them on the cross. But the Savior continues to call His church to share both His words of Law and His words of Gospel so that through this proclamation the Holy Spirit might continue to work to bring people to faith. Jesus' love for us motivates and empowers us to carry out His Great Commission as He promises to bless our work in His name.

Objectives

By the power of the Holy Spirit working through God's Word we will
1. confess the times when motivated by sin we reject God's will for our lives;
2. praise God for the forgiveness He won for our sin through Jesus' death on the cross;
3. carry out Jesus' Great Commission with renewed zeal and vigor.

Opening Worship

Sing or speak together stanza 1 of "Hark, the Voice of Jesus Calling."

Hark, the voice of Jesus calling,
"Who will go and work today?
Fields are white and harvests waiting,
Who will bear the sheaves away?"
Loud and long the Master calls you;
Rich reward He offers free.
Who will answer, gladly saying,
"Here am I. Send me, send me"?

Introduction

Rejected!

1. Tell about a time when you or someone you know has shared God's love in Jesus with an unbeliever only to have the message rejected.

2. How did you or the other person respond to the rejection?

At times we may walk away from such an experience feeling self-righteous because we at least "have not rejected Jesus." We may even feel better than those who have rejected Jesus. But the reality is that every time we sin, we reject Jesus. We are in need of hearing the same message of love and forgiveness—over and over and over again—that an unbeliever needs to hear.

3. How does the fact that your sin is open rejection of Jesus affect the attitude you have toward those who reject the message of Jesus' love and forgiveness?

4. How does Jesus' constant love and forgiveness for your rejection motivate you as you reach out to unbelievers?

In today's lesson, Jesus faces opposition and rejection. But in His love for all people Jesus continues to call sinners to repentance so that they might receive the saving faith He offers freely.

Inform

Reading the Text

The time of preparation has been completed; the servant of the Lord is ready to go to work. That work is first of all to get people ready for God's kingdom. By preaching, teaching, healing, reaching and training Jesus heralds the coming of God's rule. When asked when the kingdom of God would come, Jesus responds: "The kingdom of God is among you" (Luke 17:21). He himself brings the kingdom. He invites all to enter by trusting in him as the Savior.

Galilee is the scene of this early ministry. Jesus had grown up in this northern province ruled by Herod. In many ways it had felt the influence of the Romans and other gentiles much more than the Jewish area around Jerusalem. Consequently Galileans were treated with some disdain by the religious leadership in the south.

The Jesus who returned to Galilee was charged with the power of the Spirit. At his baptism he had heard the voice of his Father; the Spirit rested upon him; in the desert he had defeated Satan. In no time at all news about him and his activities spread through the whole countryside. He went into the village synagogues to teach the people. These synagogues were the buildings where the people assembled for worship and study of the Old Testament. Everywhere Jesus was praised. ...

Jesus was in Nazareth on the Sabbath day. As he had so often done in the past, Jesus went into the village synagogue on that day. The synagogue service included the reading of the Old Testament law and prophets. Jesus was handed the scroll of the Prophet Isaiah and read Isaiah 61:1, 2. The words were those of the servant of the Lord who declared that the Spirit was on him. He had been anointed to preach good news to the poor, to open the eyes of the blind, to release the oppressed, to proclaim the year of the Lord's favor.

68

When Jesus had finished the reading, he rolled up the scroll and handed it back to the attendant. Already his reading of this passage must have deeply impressed the people for their eyes were fixed on him as he sat down to expound this Scripture. His words at first pleased them: "Today this scripture is fulfilled in your hearing." The age of the Messiah has dawned; the servant of the Lord has come.

But gradually the implications of what Jesus was saying struck home. He himself was that servant of the Lord who had been anointed with the Spirit. His ministry was to preach and teach and heal. This was too much for these people; they knew the identity of the one saying these things: "Isn't this Joseph's son?"

The home town people had not known this man to be a miracle worker when he was among them. Rumors had come of some healings performed by Jesus in Capernaum; but these people of Nazareth needed convincing that Jesus was anything more than a rather precocious Bible student. Jesus makes reference to their doubts in a well-known proverb which asks the doctor to prove his wares by doing some healing.

No healings are forthcoming from Jesus. Rather he declares that his ministry is one much wider than simply to impress people back home. He cites two well-known Old Testament stories about the prophets Elijah and Elisha. Elijah is sent to help a non-Israelite widow survive the severe famine though there were many suffering widows at home (1 Kings 17:7–24). Elisha heals the gentile general Naaman though there were many lepers in Israel (2 Kings 5:1–19).

The people at once caught the implications of what Jesus was saying. They needed to break out of the narrow view of the Messiah that he was coming only to establish an earthly kingdom for the Jews. The servant of the Lord came to seek and to save the lost wherever they might be and whoever they were. This was too much for the Nazarenes. Filled with fury they drove their native son from the town, took him to the brow of the hill on which the town was built intent on throwing him down from the cliff. …

But the time for Jesus to die is not yet. Making use of his divine power, he walked right through the crowd and went on his way. Jesus does not go elsewhere because he rejected the people of Nazareth. Rather the people reject him because of his implied announcement that he is going elsewhere. Later the people of Capernaum had the same reaction when Jesus left their presence: they tried to keep him for themselves (4:42). The answer of Jesus: "I must preach the good news of the kingdom of God to the other towns also, because that is why I was sent."

This story of the rejection in Nazareth is a preview of a whole series of rejections which Jesus would experience. "He came to that which was his own, but his own did not receive him" (John 1:11). The stubborn self-centeredness and pride of people continues to resist the good news of the kingdom of God. Only the power of the Spirit through the Word of God overcomes the resistance and leads to faith in Jesus Christ as Savior.

(From The People's Bible Commentary: Luke © 1988 Northwestern Publishing House, Milwaukee, WI. Used by permission.)

Discussing the Text

1. Although impressed by Jesus' exposition of Scripture, why did the people quickly turn against Him?

2. Why did Jesus use His divine power to walk through the crowd?

3. How is the account of Jesus' rejection in Nazareth a preview of the rejection that was to come?

Connect

The human condition has not changed since the Garden of Eden. Like Adam and Eve, we are fallen creatures, separated from God because of our rebellion and disobedience. All people by nature are poor before God, imprisoned by sin, blind to the truth, and oppressed by our inability to save ourselves. God's holy law confronts us with a fatal reality: we are, on our own, dead in transgressions and sins (Ephesians 2:1). But Jesus is the "preacher" of Good News (Luke 4:18). His Word proclaims God's eternal plan to save sinful humanity through His Son—a plan Jesus fulfills in person, among His people, through His life, death, and resurrection.

Jesus' message today, like 2,000 years ago, often meets with opposition. The Savior calls His church, both pastors and members, to share His word of forgiveness and life with the world. Yet men, women, and children alike reject His Good News for many reasons. At times His messengers also suffer hardship or endure persecution for their efforts, as did their Lord. The Lord promises always, though, to bless our labor in His name. He gives us strength to carry out His Great Commission.

1. What evidence can you provide that God's Word continues to be rejected even today?

2. At times we may feel self-righteous—"Thank God, I am not like those sinners." Whenever we sin we reject Jesus. Knowing that you are a sinner who continually rejects Jesus, how does this affect the way you approach other sinners with the message of God's love and forgiveness through faith in Christ Jesus?

3. "Chief of sinners though I be." This line from a familiar hymn is sung often with little regard for the message. What does confessing that you are the "chief of sinners" for whom Jesus died provide you as you share His Law and His Gospel with others?

4. Write a prayer confessing your sinful rejection of Jesus. Then include a petition giving praise and thanks to God that in spite of your sin Jesus died for you. Be prepared to share the prayer during closing worship.

Vision

To Do This Week

Family Connection

1. Discuss rejection you have faced. How does it feel to be rejected?

2. How do we reject Jesus when we sin?

3. Jesus continues to invite those who have rejected Him by their sin to "Come" and receive the forgiveness only He can provide. How will Jesus' love for us motivate us to love those who reject us?

4. Discuss the words of the hymn "Chief of Sinners Though I Be." What do these words mean to you?

Personal Reflection

1. Reach out to those whom you might consider unlovable. Share concern for them so that God might provide you an opportunity to share His love for them.

2. Read daily the first stanza of "Chief of Sinners" included in the closing worship.

Closing Worship

Sing or speak together stanza 1 of "Chief of Sinners Though I Be."
> Chief of sinners though I be,
> Jesus shed His blood for me,
> Died that I might live on high,
> Lives that I might never die.
> As the branch is to the vine,
> I am His, and He is mine.

Pray aloud the prayers written earlier during the session.

For Next Week

Read Luke 5:1–11 in preparation for the next session.

Session 10

Jesus Helps Peter Catch Fish

(Luke 5:1–11)

Focus

Theme: Cast Out Your Nets!

Law/Gospel Focus

We by nature were alienated from God. But in Jesus we have a Savior, who acted on our behalf by receiving the punishment we deserved because of our sin. Jesus won forgiveness for us on the cross and renews us with His love so that we are fully equipped to labor as His servants to proclaim His Good News to all people.

Objectives

By the power of the Holy Spirit working through God's Word we will

1. confess our alienation from God because of sin and the forgiveness Jesus won for us on the cross;
2. praise God for equipping us to serve Him;
3. seek new ways to proclaim His Good News to a sin-lost world.

Opening Worship

Sing or speak together these stanzas of "Send Now, O Lord, to Every Place."

> Send now, O Lord, to ev'ry place
> Swift messengers before Your face,
> The heralds of Your wondrous grace,
> Where You Yourself will come.

> To bring Good News to souls in sin,
> The bruised and broken hearts to win;

In ev'ry place to bring them in
Where You Yourself will come.

Gird each one with the Spirit's sword,
The sword of Your own deathless Word,
And make them conqu'rors, conqu'ring Lord,
Where Your Yourself will come.

Introduction

"Cast out your nets!"

Jesus continues to command us to cast out our nets to tell others of His love for us.

1. Why do we often find it difficult to cast out our nets to those who are lost in their sin?

2. Who cast out his/her net so that you who were separated from God by sin could enjoy the blessings of forgiveness and eternal life you now possess by God's grace through faith in Jesus?

In today's lesson we witness Peter's doubt as Jesus tells him to cast out his nets. We then will experience with Peter the forgiveness Jesus provides to all sinners, including those who doubt His Word, and the power His love provides so that we can cast our nets with confidence to those who do not know His love and forgiveness.

Inform

Reading the Text

The gospel of Luke alone relates the story of Jesus' call to Peter and the miraculous catch of fish. (The gospel of John reports a second miraculous catch of fish after our Lord's resurrection, John

21:1–11.)

The "Lake of Gennesaret" (Luke 5:1) is another name for the Sea of Galilee. (The large plain south of Capernaum was probably called Gennesaret.) Jesus is teaching on the shore, near the village of Capernaum. Because of the vast crowds, Jesus uses a boat as a dock, a platform to provide a suitable distance from His audience, since words carry better over water than land.

The boat belongs to Simon, Andrew's brother (v. 3; see also John 1:40). Earlier Jesus had stayed at Simon's home and healed Simon's mother-in-law (4:38–39). In time, Simon, who is given the name Peter ("the Rock"), will become the leader of the 12 apostles and of the Christian church in Jerusalem.

When Jesus finishes teaching the people, He instructs Peter to go to deep water and "let down the nets for a catch" (v. 4). Perhaps the command seems strange to Peter, the experienced fisherman, for fish were usually caught near the shore between sunset and sunrise. Peter voices his doubt: together with his partners he has "worked hard all night" with no success (v. 5). In the light of the day, he well knows, it is unlikely that they will catch any fish. Yet for all his misgivings, Peter obeys the command. Jesus' word has authority. He has already demonstrated His power over nature by healing the sick and casting out demons (4:40–41). Now Jesus calls Peter to believe His word of mercy and divine goodness.

Simon launches the boat into the deep water. The results are extraordinary—so many fish fill the nets that the boats are in danger of sinking because of the number and weight. At once, Simon Peter recognizes the truth: he stands in the presence of God's Messiah, the Lord of the universe who commands the forces of nature. As a mere man, he might bow in humble reverence. But Peter is not simply mortal; he is unworthy. He kneels in front of Jesus. "Go away from me, Lord; I am a sinful man" (v. 8). Peter realizes his abject poverty before the Lord. He is overcome by the strength of Jesus' grace and righteousness, and in sharp contrast, his own weakness and failures.

Jesus, in turn, extends His word of comfort and pardon. He speaks as only God speaks. "Don't be afraid" is God's greeting to His anxious people (see, for example, Genesis 15:1; Joshua 11:6; Luke 1:13, 30). Jesus is the Son of God, the almighty Lord who reveals His mercy and salvation to sinful human beings. He calls men and women from the empty waters to the rich harvest of righteousness and eternal life. He also equips His followers to join in the work: "from now on you will catch men" (Luke 5:10). Peter, James, John, and the rest of the disciples now enter the ministry of the kingdom to bring other people into God's redemptive love. Without delay, they leave everything to follow Jesus (v. 11).

Discussing the Text

1. What causes Peter to doubt Jesus' instruction to go to deep water and "let down the nets for a catch"?

2. What causes Peter to do as Jesus instructs even though he doubts?

3. Why does Peter say, "Go away from me, Lord; I am a sinful man"?

4. What is the significance of Jesus' words, "Don't be afraid"?

5. Describe the significance of Jesus' words, "from now on you will catch men"? How does Jesus equip His disciples for this task?

Connect

Like Peter, we know our failures. We know our past, a "history" stained by disobedience to God, guilt, and shame. By nature we are alienated from God, separated from His holiness and opposed to His will for His creation. But also like Peter, we have a Lord and Savior, who speaks His word of compassion and comfort to repentant hearts. Jesus releases us from the past, daily forgives us, and renews us with His love.

Just as the disciples did not by their effort cause the fish to enter the nets, so we cannot by our own power cause people to enter the kingdom of God. Peter and the apostles relied on God's Word and Spirit for guidance and power in their work. We, too, rely on God's Word and Spirit. Moreover, The disciples did not sit around and watch opportunities pass by. As they had toiled with nets to catch fish, so also they labored in God's kingdom as His servants, proclaiming the Good News of Jesus in towns and cities across the Mediterranean world. As fishers of people, we also carry out our work in the presence of the Lord Jesus. We are always conscious of our unworthiness and sin, but we look to the Savior's love and mercy in all circumstances.

1. What evidence can you provide that often we doubt Jesus' command to cast out our nets to catch men?

2. When we acknowledge our failures to tell others of Jesus' love, what impact do Jesus' words, "Don't be afraid," have on us?

3. How does Jesus continue to equip us today? See 2 Timothy 3:14–17.

Vision

To Do This Week

Family Connection

1. Discuss how God can use you to be fishers of people.
2. Explain why it is sometimes dificult to "cast out your nets."
3. Pray that God would use each member of your family to share boldly God's love for you in Jesus.

Personal Reflection

1. Identify a friend or loved one who doesn't yet confess Jesus as Lord and Savior. Make a point to demonstrate love and concern to that person. Pray for an opportunity to share the reason for the joy and peace you possess.
2. Write "Cast out your net" on an index card. Place the index card in a conspicuous place in your home or apartment so that you will see it often.
3. Pray for those who remain separated from God because of their sin.

Closing Worship

Pray together:

Almighty God, since You have called Your church to witness that in Christ You have reconciled us to Yourself, grant that by Your Holy Spirit we may proclaim the Good News of Your salvation that all who hear it may receive the gift of salvation, through Jesus Christ, our Lord. Amen.

(From Lutheran Worship, copyright © 1982 by Concordia Publishing House. All rights reserved.)

For Next Week

Read Mark 5:21–43; John 11:1–44; and 1 Corinthians 15:12, 16–20 in preparation for the next session.

Session 11

Jesus Shows His Power over Death

(Mark 5:21–43; John 11:1–44; 1 Corinthians 15:12, 16–20)

Focus

Theme: Fallen Asleep!

Law/Gospel Focus

Death is our common destiny. "The wages of sin is death." But Jesus came to earth to receive the punishment of death we deserved because of our sin. When Jesus arose from the dead, He proclaimed victory for us over sin and death. For us whom He has called to faith, we have the assurance that when we fall asleep in death we will awaken to a new life with Him in heaven. His promise of eternal life motivates and empowers us to tell others of the victory Jesus won for us.

Objectives

By the power of the Holy Spirit working through God's Word we will

1. describe details concerning the accounts of the raising of Jairus' daughter and Lazarus;
2. compare the two accounts;
3. confess Jesus as the victor over death;
4. explain how Christians fall asleep in death and awaken to new life;
5. tell others of the new life Jesus won for them through His life, death, and resurrection.

Opening Worship

Sing or speak together these stanzas of "I Know that My Redeemer Lives."

> I know that my Redeemer lives!
> What comfort this sweet sentence gives!
> He lives, He lives, who once was dead;
> He lives, my everliving head!
>
> He lives and grants me daily breath;
> He lives, and I shall conquer death;
> He lives my mansion to prepare;
> He lives to bring me safely there.

Introduction

1. How important is sleep to you? Why?

2. Why is sleep so important to people?

In today's lesson Jesus confronts death—the death of Jairus' daughter and Lazarus. In both accounts, Jesus tells family and loved ones the person has "fallen asleep."

3. Why is the "falling asleep" in death so important for Christians? Why is the comparison of death to sleep so appropriate for Christians?

In this lesson we will discover the answer to these questions and others.

Inform

Reading the Text

Read aloud Mark 5:21–43; John 11:1–44; and 1 Corinthians 15:12, 16–20.

> Praise be to the Lord, to God our Savior,
>> who daily bears our burdens.
> Our God is a God who saves;
>> from the Sovereign LORD comes escape from death.
> (Psalm 68:19–20)

Escape from death? No one eludes the Grim Reaper. Or at least not under ordinary circumstances.

Jesus, however, offers the only hope of escape. He is the Lord of "both the dead and the living" (Romans 14:9), the Living Savior, who was dead and is alive forever and ever, who holds the keys of death and Hades (Revelation 1:18). In His earthly ministry, Jesus revealed His almighty power over death by raising the dead to life. His miracles showed Him to be the Son of God, who would triumph over the grave once for all in His own resurrection.

Mark 5:21–24, 35–43. Jesus is a popular teacher. Large crowds follow Him from village to village, and they spread His reputation to all the surrounding regions. Jesus is known throughout the land as a prophet, a sage, and a healer. His healing ministry in particular probably attracted many different types of people, including some leading citizens.

Jairus is a distinguished man. A ruler of the synagogue, he is a lay official who organizes and supervises worship services on behalf of the community. As a patron of religious life, Jairus also enjoys a high standing among his fellow Jews; he probably carried out other important social and political functions as well.

Jairus pleads with Jesus: Come and heal my dying daughter (v 23). For Jairus, the stakes could not be higher. Disease and sickness were always serious in the ancient world. Infection and fever could strike at any time, and a healthy individual—man, woman, or child—could be near death in a matter of hours or days. Instead of sending a delegation, Jairus personally comes to Jesus. He has no claim on the Teacher, no right to make demands or wield his influence. Jairus is a beggar. He falls at Jesus' feet with the humblest of petitions: "Put Your hands on her so that she will be healed and live" (v. 23).

Jesus responds with action. He immediately follows Jairus, though on the way He encounters and heals a woman with another grievous illness. The delay allows friends of Jairus to arrive with tragic news. The little girl has died; it is no longer necessary to "bother the teacher" (v. 35). No one escapes death, it seems. Jairus has lost his precious daughter. But the messengers' report is not the final word for Jesus. "Don't be afraid; just believe," He tells the synagogue ruler (v. 36). Believe what? Believe the other reports Jairus has heard: lepers cured, the lame walking, the blind granted sight, the deaf able to hear—believe that the demon-possessed are set free from slavery to Satan! believe that the Teacher from Nazareth has unique powers, even powers over life and death. Jesus sets out again for Jairus' home.

A "commotion, with people crying and wailing loudly," greeted Jesus and His disciples (v. 38). Ancient people typically responded to death with open displays of emotion and grief. Jesus responds with His own outcry: "The child is not dead but asleep" (v. 39). In Jesus' hands, death is mere sleep. The girl's return to life is as certain and real as waking up at the morning's first light.

Though the crowd laughs at Him, Jesus is not deterred. In the presence of His trusted disciples and the child's parents, He speaks His almighty word. Death is turned aside; God's promise to save is fulfilled here in the Messiah. Jesus then orders the witnesses "not to let anyone know about this" (v. 43), a precaution against the misguided whims of the Galilean crowds.

John 11:1–44. The raising of Lazarus of Bethany is the last miraculous "sign" in the gospel of John (see the introduction to session 7). Mary, Martha, and Lazarus are Jesus' friends. When Lazarus becomes ill, the sisters naturally look to Jesus to use His divine power to heal their brother. But Jesus sees Lazarus's illness as an opportunity to demonstrate the truth of His teaching on life and death. It is an illness that will result, not in death, but in God's glory, glory revealed first and foremost in God's Son (v. 4).

Jesus loves Lazarus (v. 3) and his family (v. 5). His delay in traveling to Bethany is then, perhaps, surprising to the disciples. When Jesus does resolve to go to Lazarus, the disciples fear for His life. (They may have assumed that Jesus, too, was initially fearful, and that He only decided to leave for Bethany with much reluctance.) The Teacher, however, knows "all things" (John 16:30). He alone knows the Father's purpose. His mission takes place now, that is, in the "hours of daylight" that the Father has granted humankind to see and believe in the Son. The disciples' anxiety is premature; the "hour" of danger—suffering and death—has not yet come. Jesus works, then, while it is still day. In the darkness of night He will not "work," but will offer Himself as a sacrifice for the sin of the world.

Jesus' statement, "Our friend Lazarus has fallen asleep" (v. 11), is completely misunderstood. The disciples think that Lazarus has found a much-needed restful slumber, an indication that he is on the road to recovery. The reality is, of course, the exact opposite. Jesus must speak bluntly and unambiguously. The time has arrived to demonstrate the truth of His word, "The dead will hear the voice of the Son of God and those who hear will live" (John 5:25).

"In the tomb for four days" (v. 17) is an indisputable sign that Lazarus is dead. In the ancient world generally, and especially in warm climates where bodies were not normally embalmed, burial took place on the day of death. Most tombs were located outside the walls of a city or village, for both ritual and hygienic reasons. The period of mourning could last up to 30 days; during this time, friends and relatives visited the family to express their sympathy and support. Martha and Mary were likely at the burial site when they heard of Jesus' imminent arrival.

Martha is first to express her faith in God's promise. Her statement to Jesus (v. 22) implies that she expects a miraculous sign, although she makes no direct request to the Lord. At a minimum, Martha affirms "the resurrection at the last day" (v. 24), the future judgment of God. Jesus, however, is the resurrection. Whoever believes in Him never really "dies," that is, never really experiences separation from God and eternal lostness. In Jesus, eternal life with the heavenly Father is a present reality.

Mary, too, meets Jesus on the way; she immediately escorts Him, along with other mourners, to the tomb. Jesus is "deeply moved in spirit and troubled" (v. 33), angry at the sight of human anguish caused by death and Satan. His command, "Take away the stone" (v. 39), is likely taken as a request to view the body of Lazarus one last time. Martha objects; the harsh facts of death will be all too apparent if the stone is rolled away. But for Jesus the glory of God is waiting to be revealed, openly, mysteriously to the eyes of faith.

The cry in "a loud voice" announces the defeat of death and Satan. Jesus proves what He says: He is the Resurrection and the Life.

Discussing the Text

1. Compare the account of raising Jairus' daughter to the account of raising Lazarus from the dead. Identify similarities and differences.

2. Jesus waits until both Jairus' daughter and Lazarus are dead before visiting the family. Why do you suppose He didn't go to each while they were sick, instead of waiting until they were dead?

3. What does Jesus' reaction to Lazarus' death tell us about Him?

4. How is "fallen asleep" an appropriate statement concerning the death of the faithful?

Connect

Death is our common destiny. St. Paul's word are true: "The wages of sin is death" (Romans 6:23). A little girl and adult man both died because they shared in, as we do also, Adam's rebellion against God. The gift of God, however, is forgiveness and peace in Christ. The Lord Jesus calls us from the darkness of death into the light of His mercy and salvation. He shows His power by calling us to faith and rescuing us from sin, death, and Satan. At the Last Day He will display His ultimate power by raising our bodies to eternal life.

Today is the "day" to work. Day and night refer to the two distinctive realms of life—God's and Satan's. Faith, grace, salvation, and eternal life characterize the "day," the time of light. Sin, unbelief, and death belong to the darkness and night. The presence of Jesus on earth constituted the time of light; His Good News still radiates with His power and love. He commissions us to continue His work, serving Him by sharing His Good News with people living in "the night."

1. What common destiny do all people share? What common destiny do all Christians share as they anticipate their death?

2. What comforting words do you find in each of the Gospel accounts?

3. What words of comfort does St. Paul provide you in 1 Corinthians 15:12, 16–20?

4. Why is there such an urgency suggested in each of the accounts?

5. Write a prayer of thanksgiving for the gift of eternal life God provides you through faith in Christ Jesus. Be prepared to share the prayer during closing worship.

Vision

To Do this Week

Family Connection

1. Discuss death. Allow time for family members to express their feelings.

2. Why is "falling asleep" an appropriate saying for Christians to use when describing death.

3. Pray together, thanking God for the eternal life He provides to all who believe in Jesus.

4. Ask, "What will heaven be like?" Allow family members to share.

Personal Reflection

1. Reread the texts from this lesson. Meditate on the magnitude of God's love for you.

2. Share God's Word of peace with someone who has recently lost a friend or loved one.

3. Pray that the Lord would provide you an opportunity to share His love for you and all people with a person who remains lost in the darkness of his/her sin.

Closing Worship

Pray the prayers of thanksgiving written earlier in this session.

For Next Week

Read John 14:1–14 and Luke 9:28–36 in preparation for the next session.

Session 12

Jesus Is the Way to the Father

(John 14:1–14; Luke 9:28–36)

Focus

Theme: What Is the Way?

Law/Gospel Focus

All people are lost in sin and unable to find their way. We cannot by our own "reason and strength" know God's truth and live according to His will. In and through the person and work of Jesus God provides the way to forgiveness and eternal life. United in Baptism to Jesus, we walk with Him toward heaven, confident in His goodness and secure in His love. His love empowers us to confess Jesus is "the Christ of God" to others who remain lost in their sin.

Objectives

By the power of the Holy Spirit working through God's Word we will

1. summarize what we learn from the two accounts about Jesus—the Way, the Truth, and the Life;
2. describe the way that Jesus reconciled the world to God;
3. express confidence in Jesus' love as we walk with Him toward heaven;
4. confess boldly to others lost in sin that Jesus is the Christ—the way to heaven.

Opening Worship

Speak together the Second Article of the Apostles' Creed and Luther's explanation.

And in Jesus Christ, His only Son, our Lord, who was conceived by the Holy Spirit, born of the Virgin Mary, suffered under Pontius Pilate, was crucified, died and was buried. He descended into hell. The third day He rose again from the dead. He ascended into heaven and sits at the right hand of God, the Father Almighty. From thence He will come to judge the living and the dead.

What does this mean? I believe that Jesus Christ, true God, begotten of the Father from eternity, and also true man, born of the Virgin Mary, is my Lord, who has redeemed me, a lost and condemned person, purchased and won me from all sins, from death, and from the power of the devil; not with gold or silver, but with His holy, precious blood and with His innocent suffering and death, that I may be His own and live under Him in His kingdom and serve Him in everlasting righteousness, innocence, and blessedness, just as He is risen from the dead, lives and reigns to all eternity. This is most certainly true.

Introduction

1. At times we all become lost. Describe a time when you or someone you know asked, "What is the way?" What was the outcome of the event?

2. Read each of the statements made by people who were asked, "What is the way to God?"
- "I'm a good person. I give to charity."
- "I've tried to live an exemplary life. That must account for something."
- "I seek God in the goodness of others."

What is wrong with each of these statements?

In the lesson for today we learn that on our own we remain lost—separated from God forever. But God in His love for us provided a "way" back to Him from sin. This "way" was accomplished for us only through the person and work of Jesus.

Inform

Reading the Text

Read aloud John 14:1–14 and Luke 9:28–36.

John 14:1–14. "Where I am going," Jesus told the disciples, "you cannot follow now, but you will follow later" (John 13:36).

Peter and his friends wanted to follow Jesus. But the Lord's journey was not to success and fame; it was to the cross.

On the night of the Passover celebration, the night He was betrayed, Jesus gathered His disciples in a large upper room in Jerusalem. There He ate the Passover feast, instituted His own meal (The Lord's Supper), and washed His disciples' feet as an illustration of humble service in the Kingdom. He also spoke at length, for the final time, about His message and His mission. He shares a farewell dinner and speech as His "testament" to the church.

The life of a disciple is, above all, a life of faith. Troubles abound. Danger threatens. Persecution awaits in the near as well as distant future. But Jesus calls His followers to faith: "Trust in God; trust also in Me" (14:1). By faith the Christian receives God's forgiveness in Jesus. By faith the Christian walks in the teachings of the Master. By faith the Christian lives as a witness and servant to the world. Apart from faith, Jesus' followers are only another band of friends, rather than a fellowship of saints in the living Savior.

Jesus has come to reveal the Father's heart to His creation. God desires to save all people. He has prepared a place of glory for the redeemed to spend eternity. It is like a "house," a mansion with many rooms (v. 2). The Father welcomes everyone, and He has sent His own Son to earth to share His Good News, the promise of eternal life through Jesus.

Jesus, in fact, is almost ready to return to the Father to prepare a place for His brothers and sisters, His church. The hour of salvation is at hand. Over the next three days Jesus will die, rise again, show Himself alive, and commission His disciples—His apostles—to carry on His work. At the cross, the work of redemption will be "finished" (John 19:30). At the resurrection, His sacrifice will be vindicated; death will be defeated. And shortly afterward, He will ascend to heaven, to prepare the Father's house to receive His beloved children. This is "the way" to the place Jesus is going (14:4).

Thomas needs assurance. He is uncertain of Jesus' "destination," and therefore does not know "the way" (v. 5). In response, Jesus makes exclusive claims. To know Jesus is to know the Father. To trust in God is to trust in Jesus. To know Jesus is also to know the way to the Father, to the Father's house. Jesus is the Way. By His atoning work all people can approach the Father (Hebrews 10:10–23). Jesus is the Truth. His Word is sure, trustworthy, God's eternal truth. Jesus is the Life. He lays down His life and takes it up again, that He may give life to all believers.

"Show us the Father and that will be enough for us" (v. 8). Philip makes one last attempt to bring God into focus, into view. Jesus, in turn, discloses the mystery of God in the world. Is God so far above that humans cannot grasp Him? No! Jesus is Immanuel, "God with us" (Matthew 1:23). He alone, who was once at the Father's side, has made the Father known (John 1:18). Jesus shows the Father to the world in three distinct ways. (1) Christ is "in" the Father and the Father is in Christ. The Father and the Son are one in unity and purpose (John 10:30). (2) Christ reveals the Father by His words. As true God, He speaks with the absolute authority of the Father (10:17–18). (3) The work of Christ is the Father's work. Christ reveals the Father in His miraculous power and sacrificial love (10:32–38).

Can disciples really do "greater things" (14:12) than Jesus? Yes, for Christ has not ascended into heaven to leave His followers without strength and direction. He goes to the Father to rule the universe as the risen Lord, who promises to hear the prayers of His people and answer according to His purpose. Jesus works through His church to carry out the greatest miracle: to bring others to saving faith.

Luke 9:28–36. The immediate context to the Transfiguration is Peter's confession of Jesus as the Messiah. The setting is the region of Caesarea Phillipi (see Matthew 16:13). This region, 25 miles northeast of the Sea of Galilee, was known for its beauty, fertility, and pagan practices. In a place where Caesar or other pagan deities were hailed as "Lord," Jesus reveals His true identity as Christ, the Lord (see Luke 2:11).

"Who do the crowds say I am?" (9:18). All human answers fall short. "John the Baptist" prepared people's hearts, but he was not the king of the Kingdom. "Elijah" was viewed as the forerunner and herald of Christ (see Malachi 4:5), but his mission was fulfilled by John (see Luke 7:18–35; Matthew 11:14). Jeremiah (see Matthew 16:14) was a bold prophet and patient sufferer who pointed forward to the new covenant (Jeremiah 31:31–34). "One of the prophets" may have included any of Israel's great spokesmen for God.

Peter, by inspiration of the Spirit of God, gives the only answer. "The Christ of God" is the Messiah, anticipated in the Scriptures and now revealed in person. But Jesus is the suffering Christ, who will travel to Jerusalem to be rejected and killed by the religious leaders. His death will be the salvation of the world, even as His resurrection will be the world's one hope for eternal life.

The Transfiguration occurs some "eight days" after Peter's confession and Jesus' disclosure of His upcoming death and resurrection. Peter, John, and James accompany Jesus to a mountain to pray (9:28). Together these three disciples form an intimate group, the Lord's most trusted friends and followers (see, for example, Luke 8:51). Jesus is transfigured, that is, "the appearance of His face changed, and His clothes became as bright as a flash of lightning" (9:29). The majesty and glory of God now shine through Jesus' human form.

"Moses and Elijah" talk with Jesus about His "departure," His death (v. 31). Moses is the deliverer of God's people from slavery in Egypt and God's spokesman to the nation; he brings God's revelation (the Law and the Ten Commandments) to the covenant people. Elijah is Israel's prophet, who speaks God's word of judgment upon an idolatrous people. Moses' face shone when he came down from Mount Sinai (Exodus 34:29). Elijah heard the Lord in "a gentle whisper" on Mount Horeb (1 Kings 19:12–13). Both ended their lives under God's care and protection. They appear here with Jesus as representative figures of God's covenant promises to His people Israel.

Peter speaks first. He proposes to build "three shelters" (9:34) for the Lord and the two ancient prophets. The suggestion is, in effect, to make a new "tabernacle," a place of meeting where God "lived" among His people to reveal His Word and ways. But Peter misunderstands the purpose of the Transfiguration. God no longer requires a movable tent, a portable sanctuary to live among His people. God has made His dwelling on earth in His Son (John 1:14). He has revealed His glory in the face of Christ to bring to light His rich mercy and salvation. As the cloud appears—also a symbol of the presence of God

(Exodus 13:21)—the voice of God attests Jesus' unique status and authority: "This is My Son, whom I have chosen; listen to Him" (Luke 9:35). As at His baptism, Jesus is revealed as God in the flesh, Immanuel.

The three disciples are naturally "afraid" (9:34). Fear always seizes sinful mortals in the presence of God. Under cover of the cloud Moses and Elijah vanish. Peter, John, and James watch, listen, but keep the event private. Only later could they proclaim the majesty of the transfigured Lord.

The Transfiguration has special significance in Jesus' life. Moses represents the Law; Elijah, the prophets. Moses gave God's law to the people. Elijah lived at a time when Israel was serving the false god Baal. He labored with zeal to destroy idolatry and lead the people back to God and His holy law. Neither of these men could keep the people from sinning against God's law, nor could they forgive their sins. But Moses and the prophets foretold the coming of the Messiah, who would take on Himself the sins of the people. Moses and Elijah appear on the mountain to show that Jesus is the promised Savior, who fulfills the Law and save sinners. His "exodus," His suffering and death, is God's means to redeem His creation from captivity.

Discussing the Text

1. What does Jesus reveal about Himself—His person and work—in the two accounts?

2. What does Jesus reveal about discipleship in the two accounts?

3. How important is the answer to the Jesus' question, "Who am I?" Why?

4. How is Jesus the Way? How important is it for people to know the Way? Why?

Connect

Many people today want to know "the way." There is a restless yearning to know God, to understand His truth, and to live according to His will. In reality, though, humankind is "lost." By nature we do not know the way. By our "reason and strength" we cannot know God's truth or live according to His will. Rather, God's Word reveals our deep inadequacy and inability. We are lost in sin and transgression. In Christ, however, God reveals the Way. Jesus is the one sure hope for forgiveness and eternal life. United with Him in Baptism, we walk with Him toward heaven, confident of His goodness and secure in His love.

St. Peter proclaims the meaning of the Transfiguration for believers (2 Peter 1:17–19). Jesus is our Messiah and Savior; we share in His triumph over sin and death. We look to Him in faith, not expecting a "mountaintop experience" at every turn in life, but rather listening to His Word, trusting His forgiveness and strength, gathering with His people to share in His gifts of Baptism and Holy Communion. His Word is the "shining light" to illuminate our pilgrim path. He promises us His heavenly glory as we walk in faith toward eternity.

1. What would you say to a person who wanted to know "the way"?

2. What do you mean when you confess "Jesus is the Christ"?

3. In what way did Jesus reconcile the world to God?

4. What confidence can you have, knowing that Jesus has shown you the "way"?

Vision

To Do This Week

Family Connection

1. Discuss each of the questions in the "Connect" section.

2. Review the events of the Transfiguration. How does Jesus reveal Himself to us today?

3. Pray that the Holy Spirit might provide each member of your family an opportunity to tell someone of Jesus' love. Share with your family opportunities you have this week to tell someone of Jesus' love.

Personal Reflection

1. Reread the scriptural accounts studied in this session.

2. Pray for opportunities to confess boldly that Jesus is the Christ to a friend or loved one.

3. Review the answers to the questions in the "Connect" section. How might these answers be used to share Jesus' love with friends or loved ones who do not confess Jesus as their Lord and Savior?

Closing Worship

Speak together the Third Article of the Apostles' Creed and Luther's explanation.

> I believe in the Holy Spirit, the holy Christian church, the communion of saints, the forgiveness of sins, the resurrection of the body, and the life everlasting. Amen.
>
> What does this mean? I believe that I cannot by my own reason or strength believe in Jesus Christ, my Lord, or come to Him; but the Holy Spirit has called me by the Gospel, enlightened me with His gifts, sanctified and kept me in the true faith.
>
> In the same way He calls, gathers, enlightens, and sanctifies the whole Christian church on earth, and keeps it with Jesus Christ in the one true faith.
>
> In this Christian church He daily and richly forgives all my sins and the sins of all believers.
>
> On the Last Day He will raise me and all the dead, and give eternal life to me and all believers in Christ.
>
> This is most certainly true.

For Next Week

Read Matthew 14:14–21 and Luke 10:25–37 in preparation for the next session.

Session 13

Jesus Provides for Us

(Matthew 14:14–21; Luke 10:25–37)

Focus

Theme: Our Greatest Need

Law/Gospel Focus

Our human needs are great. At times because of sin we may focus our attention on providing for our physical needs while neglecting our greatest need—the need for forgiveness of sins and eternal life. In Christ, God forgives our selfish desires and sinful habits and provides for us that which will last into eternity—life. God's great love for us compels us to love God and our neighbor.

Objectives

By the power of the Holy Spirit working through God's Word we will

1. describe how Jesus has provided for our greatest need;
2. explain what it means to love our neighbor;
3. seek new ways to love our neighbor and in so doing provide for his or her greatest need.

Opening Worship

Speak together the First Article of the Apostles' Creed and Luther's explanation.

I believe in God, the Father Almighty, Make of heaven and earth.

What does this mean? I believe that God has made me and all creatures; that He has given me my body and soul, eyes, ears, and all my members, my reason and all my senses, and still takes care of them.

He also gives me clothing and shoes, food and drink, house and home, wife and children, land, animals, and all I have. He richly and daily provides me with all that I

96

need to support this body and life.

He defends me against all danger and guards and protects me from all evil.

All this He does only out of fatherly, divine goodness and mercy, without any merit or worthiness in me. For all this it is my duty to thank and praise, serve and obey Him. This is most certainly true.

Introduction

1. List as many needs you can think of that you or people you know seek to have met.

2. How might our human needs and our striving to meet these needs at times get in the way of having our greatest need met—faith in the assurance of the forgiveness of sins and the eternal life Jesus won?

3. How might neglect of our spiritual need hamper our ability to love God and our neighbor?

In today's lesson we focus on how Jesus fulfills our needs and how we who have our greatest need fulfilled by God's grace through faith in Jesus can demonstrate His love to our neighbor.

Inform

Reading the Text

Read aloud Matthew 14:14–21 and Luke 10:25–37.

Matthew 14:14–21. As Jesus steps off the boat and onto land, He sees a great crowd with great needs. As a shepherd cares for his flock, so Jesus has "compassion" on God's people, feeding their souls with His words of life and healing their illnesses with His divine power.

As the day wears on, however, these men, women, and children also began to experience physical hunger. The compassionate Savior does not "send the crowds away," as His disciples suggest (v. 15), but He desires to satisfy their earthly needs, too.

Before feeding the crowd, however, Jesus tests the disciples: "You give them something to eat" (v. 16). The disciples fail the test. No one understands the nature of Jesus' instruction. No one recognizes that Jesus can and will provide.

"Loaves of bread" (v. 17) were large, round cakes, a few inches thick, made of wheat or barley. (The gospel of John reports that Andrew discovered the boy among the crowd; the five loaves and two fish may have been the child's lunch.)

Jesus' command to the disciples, to have the people "sit down" (v. 19), was unusual. The word normally meant "to recline for the purpose of eating a meal." Will Jesus the host serve the boy's lunch to this multitude? Jesus looks reverently toward heaven, gives thanks, breaks the loaves, and distributes His gifts, first to the disciples and then through the disciples to the people. The meal outdoors is reminiscent of God's great provision to Israel during the wilderness wandering. The meal also anticipates another holy meal, the Lord's Supper, the giving of the Messiah's body and blood for the forgiveness of sins. (The Lord's Supper, of course, points forward to the messianic feast in heaven.)

"The disciples picked up twelve basketfuls of broken pieces" (v. 20). God's abundance is more than sufficient—for all Israel. (The number 12 is likely symbolic of the 12 tribes of Israel.) Everyone eats and is satisfied. The Messiah gives life to God's hungry people.

Luke 10:25–37:

The expert in the law who stands up to put Jesus to the test is a representative of the "wise and learned" from whom the things of God remain hidden (10:21). He demonstrates his knowledge of the Old Testament Scriptures by quoting Deuteronomy 6:5 concerning love to God and Leviticus 19:18 about love for the neighbor. He gives the correct answer; Jesus directs him to do the law, to put it into practice (8:21). …

[This law expert] feels the need to "justify himself" for asking a question which had such a simple answer, one he himself easily supplied. So the lawyer asks a further question seeking to demonstrate that loving your neighbor as yourself does call for a legal definition of the term "neighbor." Generally among the Jews the neighbor was defined a fellow countryman, one of the same race.

The story which Jesus tells overturns such an understanding of the word "neighbor." … [The] Samaritan, whom the lawyer would probably have excluded from his definition of "neighbor," shows himself as the one who fulfilled the command to love one another, in this case even an enemy.

The expert in the law had asked: "Who is my neighbor?" In the parable which Jesus tells this question is answered. But Jesus goes a step further with the question he now puts to the lawyer: "Which of these three … was a neighbor?" For Jesus the real question is not who is my neighbor but how does one prove oneself a neighbor to others. … Jesus makes this hated Samaritan a model for true neighborliness. The Samaritan is one of the "little children" to whom has been revealed the hidden wisdom of God. He sees beyond the racial divisions of this world to the will of God which bids us to love the neighbor whoever that neighbor might be. … The early church saw in the Good Samaritan none other than Christ himself. No one else so radically fulfilled the love commandment. Faith in Jesus is the way to eternal life, a faith which shows its life by love for God and neighbor.

(From The People's Bible Commentary: Luke © 1988 Northwestern Publishing House, Milwaukee, WI. Used by permission.)

Discussing the Text

1. How does Jesus demonstrate His concern for people's physical needs? Why is this important for us to know?

2. How does the Messiah give spiritual life to God's hungry people?

3. How does Jesus provide for our needs in the spiritual meal He provides us—the Lord's Supper?

4. Consider the parable of the Good Samaritan. Who is your neighbor? How is this different than most people's conception of neighbor?

5. How does Jesus reveal Himself in the parable of the Good Samaritan as the true Good Samaritan?

Connect

Human needs are great. Every day we crave food and water for basic sustenance. Our spiritual needs, however, are even greater. Too often, though, we ignore the means to sustain and nourish our relationship with God. In truth, sin stands at the root of our neglect. We are satisfied with "bread for the moment," and God seems remote from our everyday cares and routines. Because the sinful nature remains in all people, we do not—and cannot properly—"fear, love and trust God above all things." In Christ, God forgives our selfish desires and sinful habits. Jesus is the Father's gift to the world, a gift that bestows life, hope, and eternal salvation through His death and resurrection. As our Good Shepherd, Jesus feeds us with His Word, with baptismal grace, and with His body and blood.

"Go and do likewise" (Luke 10:37). God's Law demands that we love, support, and show compassion to all people. By nature, we cannot keep God's command; on our own we cannot be a "Good Samaritan." Jesus, the true "Good Samaritan," has fulfilled the Law's demand in our place. His atoning sacrifice is our hope of forgiveness and the source of strength to love both God and our neighbor as He has loved us.

1. How do you often ignore or neglect the means God provides to sustain and to nourish your relationship to Him?

2. What does God continue to offer to you even as you fail to "fear, love, and trust God above all things"?

3. How might you better demonstrate love to your "neighbor"?

4. What motivates us to "Go and do likewise"?

5. Write a prayer of thanksgiving for all that God provides for you—physical and spiritual needs. Be prepared to share the prayer during closing worship.

Vision

To Do This Week
Family Connection
1. Create a family list of the many blessings God provides for you.
2. Ask, "What greatest need do we have that God has provided for? How did Jesus provide for this greatest need?
3. Discuss how your family might be better neighbors to those in need.

Personal Reflection

1. Think of a person to whom you could be a good Samaritan. Then be a good Samaritan to that person.

2. Make a list of all that God has provided to you. Then give thanks to Him for each of these blessings.

3. Develop a plan to spend more time in God's Word.

Closing Worship

Pray aloud the prayers of thanksgiving written earlier in this session.

For Next Week

Read Luke 22:7–38 in preparation for the next session.